OPERATION ORDINARY

» LIVE THE TRUTH,
» RESIST DEMOCRATIC
SOCIALISM

LEAH THAYER PRITCHARD

GIDEON HOUSE BOOKS

Operation Ordinary:

Live the Truth, Resist Democratic Socialism

© 2020 by Leah Pritchard

Published by Gideon House Books
www.gideonhousebooks.com

Unless otherwise indicated, all Scripture quotations are taken from the Holy Bible, New Living Translation, copyright © 1996, 2004, 2015 by Tyndale House Foundation. Used by permission of Tyndale House Publishers, a Division of Tyndale House Ministries, Carol Stream, Illinois 60188. All rights reserved.

ISBN: 978-1-943133-83-3

Dedicated to the memory of the 60 million and counting unborn American children our society has "eliminated" since 1973 in the name of "social progress."

∽o∾

Have mercy on me, O God...

For I recognize my rebellion;
    it haunts me day and night.
Against You, and You alone, have I sinned;
    I have done what is evil in Your sight.
You will be proved right in what You say,
    and Your judgment against me is just...

Purify me from my sins, and I will be clean;
    wash me, and I will be whiter than snow.
Oh, give me back my joy again;
    you have broken me—
    now let me rejoice.
Don't keep looking at my sins.
    Remove the stain of my guilt.
Create in me a clean heart, O God.
    Renew a loyal spirit within me.
Do not banish me from your presence,
    and don't take your Holy Spirit from me.

—EXCERPTS FROM PSALM 51

TABLE OF CONTENTS

INTRODUCTION

Of course, I didn't realize it at the time—one rarely recognizes the full significance of life events until long after they occur, but the seed of this book was planted in my soul nearly thirteen years ago when my husband Josh and I first moved overseas to teach English at a university in Southeastern China.

Our initial weeks there still pound like a drumbeat in my memory.

Every Fall all incoming freshmen are required by law to undergo military training in universities across China; regular classes don't begin for freshmen until this exercise is complete. From our third-story apartment windows, we had a bird's-eye view of our school's road, soccer field, and basketball courts which overnight were shaded in with crisp, straight lines of freshman students.

For several weeks, thousands of 18-year-olds, most of them fresh from the countryside, drilled and marched. As they circled and crossed campus in a neat formation, they shouted out counts in unison:

"Yī! Èr! Sān! Sì! Yī-èr-SĀN....sì!"
One! Two! Three! Four! One-two-THREE....four!

The sea of camo rippling eerily between the gray university buildings was unlike anything I had seen before. It was unnerving, and I wondered if the repetitive counting would drive me to insanity before the month was out. We breathed a sigh of relief each night when the marching and shouting finally ended and students were dismissed to their dorms.

The American English teachers preceding us at the university had known we were coming and left a stash of random items in boxes for us in the guest room armoire of the foreign teacher's apartment.

One afternoon soon after we arrived, we decided it was time to unpack those boxes.

The teachers had left books, teaching materials, and Christmas decorations; pots and pans, board games, and muffin mixes. We discovered, mercifully, a pair of U.S.-sized women's rain boots that came in handy during the floods that next spring; and what was to become my best friend inside our cold apartment that winter—a long, warm, puffy blue bathrobe.

We had brought only two suitcases each from America, so that closet was a gold mine.

The last box Josh and I dragged from the very back of the armoire was stuffed with more clothes from home: sweaters, shirts, flannel pants. Chinese clothes don't fit average-sized Americans, so these extra hand-me-downs were welcome.

We gathered up the clothes to lift them out of the box; but as we did so, other items began slipping out of the fabric, thudding to the floor.

Surprised, we stooped to pick them up and discovered a secret collection of books and videos—materials which were at that time either highly sensitive or completely banned by the government in China. The teachers had left us Chinese Bibles, Christian books, copies of the *Jesus Film* in Mandarin, and various censored Chinese history books—all painstakingly rolled up inside the shirts and sweaters.

Contraband.

We lined up the forbidden items on the floor and stared at them, then at each other, in disbelief.

We could lose our jobs if this stash was discovered. We could be evicted from the country.

The rigid, rhythmic marching of student soldiers-in-training outside our window continued as a blanket of responsibility silently wrapped itself around our shoulders.

We had been given a trust.

What was it in these materials the Communist government was so determined to hide from her people? What could be so dangerous?

The answer seared through our hearts like a sword:

Truth.

∽o∾

One of the items we discovered in that box was a 3-part DVD documentary series entitled *China: A Century of Revolution.*[1] This documentary, first televised on PBS, exposes the realities of the horrific oppression and upheaval the people of China endured during the socialist revolution and implementation of communism which occurred from 1911-1997. The series is shocking, raw, and not available in China.

That January, when our neighbors and students deserted the campus for Chinese New Year and the air grew so frigid inside our gray cement apartment building that our little heater couldn't compete, Josh and I watched the entire series through twice, huddled together on the couch under a pile of blankets and that puffy blue bathrobe.

I remember choking back sobs through much of the documentary, especially Part Two, which uncovers the tumultuous and inhumane Mao years. By this time I had names and faces to match with the intense hardships recounted in the film.

Gentle old āyí (auntie) with the sad face, who squats every morning in the alley peeling garlic; kind nǎi nai and yé ye (grandmother and grandfather) who have embraced me as though I were part of your family...what have your eyes seen?

9

So much chaos. So much insanity. So much raw suffering was borne by the Chinese people during that revolutionary period of China's history.

So much bitter *class struggle*.

And to what end?

That documentary shook me. It changed me.

When my beloved students returned to their overcrowded, unheated, and rat-infested dorms after the holiday—some shyly trying to hide from me their badly frostbitten cheeks—my heart broke further.

When I read their "creative" writing essays, they all sounded blank and *hauntingly the same*. It was as if a beautiful, crucial part of their brilliant minds was inaccessible even to themselves. It was locked inside an invisible prison.

The prison of communism.

Throughout the remainder of that year, and when we returned to live in a different province several years later, I kept my eyes open wide. My husband and I immersed ourselves in Chinese culture. We observed how communist propaganda worked. We listened and asked our friends many questions.

I felt driven both by compassion and by pure horror to understand communism and what is behind it and how it manages to keep the minds of millions of citizens bound.

In China, we saw something we will never be able to un-see. What we encountered was a palpable darkness intent on concealing Truth; an entire society circled by a curtain shrouding its vision and hindering its ability to think freely.

We, as Americans at that time, had access to mountains of information, facts, and resources which we found out the majority of Chinese people could neither see nor obtain. Most of them didn't even know such a broad, beautiful world of dependable facts—as well as diverse views, ideas, and information—existed.

An entire society of people was going about their lives, making decisions, and viewing life based on augmented reality; with one hand, as it were, tied behind their backs.

And so in China, we learned this most valuable lesson:

The world is not always as it seems.

Little did we know that nine years later, as Josh and I returned to America after our second move to China, we would encounter a tidal wave of change sweeping our own country that would send us reeling.

We felt the tremors of a massive cultural earthquake happening in the West.

We were horrified at the sudden realization that *the same curtain of darkness we had encountered in China*—clearly recognizable to us now—was ever so slowly, discreetly, and silently being lowered in the United States. The Land of the Free!

This time, however, we weren't standing outside the curtain looking in.

This time we were trapped inside.

What was happening to our beautiful nation?

One afternoon as I prayed with tears in my eyes for God to help me make sense of it all, old memories stirred in my mind of that cold, gray January holiday in China. Images from the Chinese Cultural Revolution documentary we had watched nine years earlier started flashing through my brain.

Suddenly, in a moment of stark clarity, I could see.

Once again, I felt the heavy weight of Truth pressing down on my shoulders. What if all we had heard, seen, learned, and experienced in China was *for such a time as this?*

God laid this verse on my heart: "Give them my entire message; include every word. Perhaps they will listen and turn from their evil ways. Then I will change my mind about the disaster I am ready to pour out on them because of their sins." Jeremiah 26:2b, 3

My friends, there is a disaster fast approaching America—and I am not talking about a tornado, a flood, or even a deadly worldwide virus.

The disaster is called socialism.

PART ONE
SOCIALISM AND THE DESTRUCTION OF ORDINARY LIVING

"This is what the Lord says: 'Stop at the crossroads and look around. Ask for the old, godly way, and walk in it. Travel its path, and you will find rest for your souls.' But you reply, 'No, that's not the road we want!'"

—JEREMIAH 6:16

1

GRAND THEFT OF AMERICA'S ORDINARY

THE SOCIALIST REVOLUTION OF AMERICA

It used to be so simple, so clear—who we are and what we stand for in this country.

One nation under God, indivisible, with liberty and justice for all.

Our Constitution. Our Bill of Rights. Our liberty. Our fierce independence. Our work ethic. Our industry. Our ingenuity. Our prosperity. Our strong families. Our respect for authority. *Our belief in God.* These things defined us as a nation.

It's not so apparent these days. It's not that simple any more. Something familiar is slipping away. Our *ordinary* is disappearing.

In the United States today, tensions are being stretched to a breaking point and it's confusing. Who are we? Where are we going? What is it that's happening?

It's not just our national identity that is disappearing. We are losing something else even more fundamental.

We are losing our identity as human beings.

Somewhere along the way, we lost our compass.

Where did we come from? Where are we now? Why do we exist? What is normal behavior for human beings? What *is* ordinary? Does anyone know?

We are all being sucked up into a great swirling mass of chaos, confusion, and pain.

In 2016, when my husband and I arrived in Dallas after two years living in China, we realized quickly that the America we once knew was disappearing. What shocked us was the fact that everywhere we looked we saw startling similarities between the words, attitudes, and actions of American society today and those which were expressed in 20th century China throughout her Communist Cultural Revolution:

There is today in the United States a *heightened awareness* of sharp dividing lines running through our society. Over the last two decades, everyone in the country has been figuratively herded into pens according to gender, race, religion, socio-economic status, and political standing. Overnight, friends have become enemies and our differences feel increasingly irreconcilable.

There's an urgency in the air to fight for an *improved society:* an "enlightened" civilization that will be marked by material equality, social justice, human fulfillment, peace, and environmental consciousness.

We are being asked to participate in a new societal practice of *labeling.* Large groups of people are collectively accused and shamed. *Uneducated, bigots, racists, climate change deniers, fascists, homophobes, xenophobes, white supremacists, nationalists, hate mongers, Islamaphobes...* The terms are perhaps not new to America, *but the ferocity and broad, indiscriminate strokes with which they are applied certainly are.*

There is a *demand for confession and reparations.* Society demands now that "the 1%", whites, conservatives, heterosexual males, and Christians stand up to apologize for their existence; for all the ways their beliefs and history have harmed and oppressed our society. After apologizing, they are then invited to stand silent because their opinions and perspectives are no longer considered relevant or valid.

Socialist policies are being more openly pushed through government channels. Single-payer healthcare, free college, public preschool, extreme environmental regulations…these are not far from becoming a reality. Openly socialist politicians are emerging on the public stage.

Older generations are surprised by the rising wave of political and socio-ethical passion of our younger generations. Millennials wear the title *"social justice warrior"* as a badge of honor and there's a growing gulf between generations.

Then there is the disconcerting *blurring of the truth* by the media. Fake news is abundant; and arguments erupt over which news is legitimate and which isn't. We don't know who or what to believe.

A fog of confusion and distrust has begun to obscure the open, free, and clear pursuit of truth to which we were formerly accustomed. Big tech companies have taken it upon themselves to block content they deem "dangerous." Major online stores have begun censoring certain books that might be "hurtful." Entertainment and nightly news are filled with blatant *propaganda.*

We see a swelling of harsh ridicule against *old ideas, old culture, old customs, and old habits.* "Capitalist" ideas. "Traditional" family culture. "Judeo/Christian" customs. "American" habits. Statues are being torn down. The American flag is offensive. Everything for which the United States of America once so proudly stood—all of our former *ordinary*—has become socially taboo and shamefully *immoral.*

If my husband and I had not lived in China, where we had devoted a substantial chunk of our lives to understanding Chinese culture and the inner workings of communism, I don't believe we would have been able to see what is happening today with such clarity.

The attitudes and events unfolding in the United States are mirror images of those that occurred last century during

China's Cultural Revolution. The more one studies socialism, the more one discovers that these are the same attitudes and actions which have surfaced time and again in socialist movements throughout history.

There is a sudden heightened awareness of class division. The shimmering promise of a better future. The choosing of scapegoats—entire groups within society—to be held responsible for all of society's evils. The labeling and shaming of those people. The demanding of confessions. The rise of a freshly-educated and fiercely passionate young generation ready to fight for equality at any cost. The appearance of socialist politicians arriving on the scene as saviors—poised and ready to liberate society from all its shameful social injustices. The general confusion about what is trustworthy information and what isn't. The increasingly pervasive propaganda in media, entertainment, and educational institutions. The all-out war against all traditional bulwarks of culture. The widespread disdain for Christianity and the Law of God.

These are undeniable trademarks of a socialist revolution.

We are at war, and we have been for a long time. We are at this moment in the middle—or maybe near the end—of a socialist revolution.

America, please hear me: We must take time to understand what this means.

In this book, I aim to dig deep into the heart of socialism—specifically *democratic socialism*—exploring what it really is and why it is more closely tied to communism and fascism than we are led to believe.

I will take a look at what democratic socialism has already cost America, and what it will, if we continue to embrace it, mean for our future.

I will also demonstrate that there is only one weapon in the world strong enough to defeat the lie of socialism. While every one of us has this weapon at our disposal, there is an important question still unanswered:

Who will have the faith and courage to use it?

"A revolution is not a dinner party, or writing an essay, or painting a picture, or doing embroidery. It cannot be so refined, so leisurely and gentle, so temperate, kind, courteous, restrained and magnanimous. A revolution is an insurrection, an act of violence by which one class overthrows another."

—MAO ZEDONG

2

LOOKING BACK AT 20TH CENTURY COMMUNISM

REVOLUTION BY VIOLENCE

The communist revolutions that took the 20th-century world by storm were revolutions of violence.

World history education in America doesn't often include enough about all that occurred in the 20th century. Many of us grew up in school learning only the most basic facts about the World Wars. World War II, for example, could be summed up as the following: Pearl Harbor happened. Nazi Germany was very bad. We dropped an atomic bomb on Japan. America and the Allies won the war.

We thankfully learned about the Holocaust and its horrors, but most of us were taught very little—if anything—about the moral ideology and politics that paved the way for a Nazi rise to power. Our education most likely also overwhelmingly failed to inform us about the staggering death and torture which also occurred last century in communist countries like China and the Soviet Union.

We have missed identifying, therefore, a common thread—a bright red thread—that can be found running all throughout the atrocious evils of last century: *socialism*.

This menacing red thread of socialism wasn't snipped off neatly at the turn of the century, as one might have hoped; but is stealthily—even as we speak—weaving itself into the fabric of our present-day lives right here in the United States.

∽o∽

China didn't lose her heart and soul to Marxism overnight.

In the early 1900s, circumstances in China had reached a boiling point. Rival warlords had divided the country and were fighting one another for power. Common people were caught in the middle of the infighting and growing unrest rippled across the nation. The country desperately needed to come together. It was becoming more and more apparent every day that serious changes had to be made.

A long and tedious tug of war ensued between the Nationalist Party and the Communist Party, which had competing ideas about what sort of changes were needed. Nationalist leaders were capitalistic in their ideals and drew support from the United States. Communist leaders followed Marxist ideals and drew their support from the Soviet Union.

For a long while, it looked as though the Nationalists would come out on top, but then things started to go awry. A long war with Japan depleted the Nationalists' energy and reserves and some of the Nationalist leaders became corrupt. Over time the Nationalists lost the trust and support of the masses and the Communist Party began to gain ground.

It was at this time that the Communist Party's carefully formulated strategy to fully win over the working class kicked into high gear. It was headed by a man named Mao Zedong—a poet, visionary, and scrupulous student of Marxist-Leninist theory.

Mao's Marxist strategy for revolution involved the following: 1) raise class consciousness, 2) cast a vision for a new and better society, 3) silence dissenters through accusation and shame, 4) demand confessions, 5) implement socialist policies, 6) respond with damage control all along the way, 7) mobilize student warriors, 8) reeducate the masses, and 9) obliterate traditional culture.[2]

Here's how it all unfolded:

1. Raise Class Consciousness

The first thing the Communists did to begin their rally for support was to raise class consciousness. They started in the cities and then fanned out throughout China holding rallies that stirred up envy, animosity, and discontentment between different groups of people.

"Raising class consciousness" is a critical concept to understand as it is a major piece of Marxist revolutionary strategy. It is the act of clearly defining classes within a society in order to move people away from *individual* thought and action toward *group* thought and action. Its aim is to heighten the public's awareness of and dissatisfaction with class differences.[3]

It involves identifying an "exploited" class, educating that class about how much they have been wronged, and blaming another "privileged" group for all the exploitation that has occurred. Raising class consciousness intentionally divides a population into clearly defined groups and pits them against each other to destabilize a capitalist society.

Life in China at that time was hardest for factory workers living in the cities, so the Communists began their rally for support there. They pointed a long, accusing finger at the middle and upper classes and the Nationalists—the "capitalists"—who were allegedly responsible for all the sufferings of the working class.

Lines of division seared through society, and seemingly overnight people woke up to find themselves grouped and placed in clearly defined, highly antagonistic corners.

2. Cast a Vision For a New and Better Society

Everywhere they went, the Communists held out to the working class a golden promise for a perfect society. This upcoming era would be one marked by equality, social justice, and relief from suffering. There would be a complete end to poverty, hunger, and exploitation.

The picture the Communists painted for China's future was breathtaking. Together, the Chinese people could create a new society that would benefit *all* people, not just the "ruling class."

Most people in China at that time didn't know much about communism. The working people just knew—thanks to the Communist Party's education—that they were being horribly oppressed. What the Communist Party was promising sounded good and felt right, so the working class banded together and began to respond with thundering enthusiasm. They rallied behind the Communists.

3. Silence Dissenters Through Accusation & Shame

The next step was for the Communists to instruct the working and peasant classes to openly accuse, criticize, and "struggle" against the capitalists in the middle and upper classes. These classes had to be educated, as well, to understand their exploitative role within society.

Hostility erupted and sparks of the revolution were fanned into a hot flame. Capitalists and those who supported the Nationalist Party were slapped with humiliating labels. They were ostracized and publicly shamed. These "rightists," imperialists," and "enemies of the State" were dragged in front of crowds and chastised in public "struggle meetings."

4. Demand Confessions

Landlords, rich farmers, counter-revolutionaries, "bad-influencers," and rightists were forced to confess their "class crimes" in these open struggle meetings. Some had been outspoken in their anti-Communist positions, but often the citizens who were "struggled against" were completely clueless as to what they had done to deserve the abuse. If a foreign-made item was discovered in one's home, for example, one was automatically held guilty for asserting one's *imperialist tendencies* and for supporting capitalism.

Many of the struggle meetings turned brutally violent: citizens who had been stamped with the negative labels were tied to posts, beaten, and in many cases killed.

This was only the beginning.

In 1949 the Nationalist Party dissolved as Nationalist leaders were forced to flee to Taiwan, and on October 1 of that year, the Communists officially took control of the country. They established The People's Republic of China and installed Mao Zedong as their leader.

The people celebrated. Finally, after so much internal fighting, China was united. The people would be in control! Poor working conditions, exploitation, and poverty would be a thing of the past.

However, what actually transpired wasn't at all what the people envisioned or what they had been promised.

Over the next 22 years, Mao began leading China through the stages of Marxist socialism at a frantic pace. His vision was set on seeing China reach the communist "utopia" Marx believed to be the glorious end of the socialist progression of a society.

Through a long series of more violent "struggles" against the capitalists, Mao and the Communist Party were able to silence all remnants of capitalist idealism and gain complete control over the Chinese people.

5. Implement Socialist Policies

The centralized government gradually took full control of land and the output of farms and factories.

National healthcare was established.

Private property was abolished.

Mao organized the people into working groups and formed farming cooperatives; later these were transformed into full-blown communes. Families and village life had always been central to Chinese culture, but these became obsolete inside the communes. Mothers were moved to factories and fields to work right alongside fathers; children were raised in communal daycares.

Initially, people were enthusiastic. Most were willing to hand over their farmland to the government because they genuinely believed they were working toward something good and right. They believed in the promises of the Communist Party. They believed in a bright future for China. They believed they were closer than ever to prosperity, equality, and true freedom.

Workers and peasants, now living in communes, worked harder for their new country and their new leader than they had ever worked before. With religious zeal, they poured blood, sweat, and tears into the building of their new equal society.

6. Run Damage Control

Mao had promised the poor an end to hunger through his socialist policies, but the policies backfired. Between 1959 and 1961 an astonishing **30-45 million[4] peasants died of starvation** as they watched truckload after truckload of grain and crops they had planted and harvested with their own bare hands being hauled away to fund Mao's socialist initiatives and to feed people living in the cities.

At least thirty million people died as a direct result of Mao's socialist policies.

No media outlets in China reported these horrors, so individual villages had no idea the starvation was so widespread. Still, the initial enthusiasm of the people evaporated as their hunger and suffering increased to levels they had never experienced before.

Mao realized that the catastrophic effects of his policies were eroding the confidence of the common people, and he began to fear that capitalist voices would re-emerge to challenge his rule.

7. Mobilize Student Warriors & Reeducate the Masses

In 1966 Mao's revolution took a dramatic new turn. Fearing that his disastrous farming policies would lead to an uprising, he abruptly turned his back on the working class and bestowed his favor and attention instead on the nation's youth. An entire generation of Chinese youth was effectively brainwashed through a nationwide Communist education movement, and these young people rose up next to push the revolution forward.

This latest "class struggle" of Mao's, which he called *The Cultural Revolution*, mobilized high school and university students to carry on the combat against the evils of immoral capitalism. Schools were transformed from centers of learning into centers of activism, and the media was converted into a socialist propaganda-spewing machine.

8. Obliterate Traditional Culture

During the Cultural Revolution, Mao entreated his student warriors to "Destroy The Four Olds":

"Old Ideas"
"Old Culture"
"Old Customs"
"Old Habits"

Groups of dedicated students who called themselves "The Red Guards" marched all around the country. They were fiercely loyal to Marxist ideals and were committed to cleansing the country of "The Four Olds."

There was a meticulous method behind Mao's madness. Marxism teaches that, in the progression of a society toward communism,

> ...as long as other classes, especially the capitalist class, still exist, as long as the proletariat [the exploited class] is still struggling with it, it must use coercive means, hence governmental means: it is still a class, and the economic conditions on which the class struggle and the existence of classes rest have not yet disappeared, and must be removed by force, or transformed, their processes of transformation must be speeded up by force.[5]

In a frenzied tide of emotion and socialist moralistic zeal, these young students turned on their own countrymen. There were more labeling and more "struggle meetings." Books were burned, temples looted, contents of museums destroyed, statues torn down. Ordinary Chinese culture was ripped from society.

Even Communist Party officials who dared question Mao's policies were beaten.

Intellectuals were tortured.

Capitalist business owners were publicly humiliated.

Religious people were flogged.

Millions of innocent people, like those listed above, were again tied to posts and forced to confess the capitalist crimes they had committed against their countrymen and against Communism.

Anyone who dared speak out against the Red Guards was labeled as "reactionary" or "imperialist" and ostracized—*or worse.*

Many offenders, including many Christian pastors, were sent to prison, and almost 400,000 people were killed in China by student groups. The students killed *four hundred thousand* of their own grandparents, neighbors, family, and friends.

It was effective.

In the end, all opposition was indeed silenced and China was united.

However, she had lost something precious indeed.

She had lost her voice, her identity, and her culture. She had lost her freedom.

There was no utopian society waiting for China at the end of the road. It had all been a lie. The problems of poverty and exploitation were worse than ever. Working conditions declined.

After all the revolution, chaos, division, death, and destruction—after all the loss and pain—China had not rid herself of injustice.

Far from it.

She woke up cold, hungry, and poor; suffocating and strangled more tightly than ever in the iron grip of oppression.

∽∘∾

Despite differences in culture, economic conditions, and speed/ methods of implementation, there are striking similarities between China's communist revolution story and what we see erupting in American society today.

In China, the attempted implementation of Marxist theories occurred openly, violently, and at breakneck speed. Here in America, they have been introduced slowly, quietly and so far—until very recently—peacefully. A dribble here, a drop there. What we have are two separate tapestries woven by the same red thread.

Dividing citizens into clearly defined class groups and fanning a hot flame of animosity between them; shaming and labeling; attacking "traditional" culture and capitalist systems; pressuring innocent people to apologize for their offenses against humanity and to conform; silencing opposing opinions through censorship and intimidation; increasing the pervasiveness of propaganda in media; transforming the education system into an instrument of political grooming; and actively controlling the flow of information, thereby obstructing the open pursuit of truth.

Socialism, dressed up in modern clothing known as "democratic socialism," is making a late but fashionable appearance in the West.

"Many who have read Marxist books have become renegades from the revolution, whereas illiterate workers often grasp Marxism very well."

—MAO ZEDONG

3

DEMOCRATIC SOCIALISM DEFINED:

THE ECONOMIC ALTERNATIVE

It's no secret that socialism's popularity is spreading rapidly in the United States, but some of us don't realize it's no longer just Bernie Sanders' followers who are embracing its ideals. Socialism has become deeply entrenched in the beliefs and goals of the Democratic Party as a whole, and many Republican Americans and politicians are adopting socialist-leaning beliefs as well.

Whether we embrace socialism or fear it, how many of us really *understand* it? No American can afford to be uneducated on this topic.

As I have learned in my research for this book, attempting to define socialism is like trying to catch a rainbow; the term is slippery and elusive. The harder one tries to nail down its precise meaning, the more evident it becomes how much even socialists themselves disagree on what that is.

To present as full and accurate a picture of modern socialism as I can, therefore, I have chosen in Part One of this book to zero in first on the basic nuts-and-bolts definitions and economics of socialism, and then to slowly pan out to examine its wider ideals, methods, history, and beliefs—illustrating how these all war against a society's ordinary culture. Then, in Part

Two we will explore in a very practical sense how socialism has affected our daily lives here in America and what we can do to reclaim our lost ordinary.

With every chapter, it is my aim to examine democratic socialism from a slightly broader perspective so that by the end we will walk away with a comprehensive picture of what it really is and what it means for America today. But any discussion of socialism must begin with economics:

Socialism vs. Capitalism: Economics 101

Socialism, according to Merriam Webster, is "any of various economic and political theories advocating collective or governmental ownership and administration of the means of production and distribution of goods."[6]

Socialism is, traditionally, an economic system in which either the government itself or all the people of a society together (the "collective") own production facilities such as factories, farms, and banks. Government bureaucracies *plan* the economy and take over economic decisions such as which goods are produced and at what quantity, how much goods and services cost, and how these products or services are distributed among consumers.

The economic alternative to socialism is of course **capitalism**, a system in which individual private citizens and corporations—rather than either the government or the "people" collectively —own and administer the means of production (factories, farms, banks, etc.).

In a pure capitalist system, the government's role in economics is extremely limited. Its job is primarily to set and enforce overarching laws to ensure that everyone in the free market must abide by the same "rules of the game." Individual producers, then, are free to decide on their own how much of their own capital and energy they are willing to risk in the market to make a profit. Individual consumers are free to make their own decisions about what they value most, where they want to spend their hard-earned money, and how much they are willing to pay for various goods and services. Under capitalism, this "free market" relationship between producers and consumers is what dictates which goods and services are produced, at what quantity, and at what cost.

The basic differences between socialism and capitalism could be summarized as the following:

Socialism values *government* ownership/regulation of the means of production; capitalism values *private* ownership of the means of production.

Socialism desires *government control* over the economy; capitalism desires *free market* control with limited government involvement.

Socialism values *collective* rights; capitalism values *individual* rights.

Theories of Value

Socialism and capitalism also rest on two opposing economic theories of value. Karl Marx, one of the fathers of modern socialism, made sweeping accusations against capitalism and claimed it was an inherently unjust and oppressive system. His conclusions to that end were based on what economists call the *labor theory of value*. This theory states that the value of an item is *inherent in the makeup of the item*. It states that value corresponds directly with an item's physical properties plus the amount of labor needed to produce it.

If the labor theory of value is true, it follows that the price of any item should directly correspond with the cost of materials plus the amount of labor put into making the product. It becomes *immoral*, then, for the owner(s) of a company to take home any profit over and above that amount. According to this labor theory, workers deserve an equal share of *all* profits. A boss who pockets any amount of profit—especially a large profit!—over and above what he pays his workers is guilty of gross exploitation. The boss is stealing from his workers what is rightfully theirs.

President Obama made a memorable statement in a 2012 campaign speech that perplexed many Americans. It makes sense, though, when understood within the context of the labor theory of value. Obama said, "If you've got a business, you didn't build that."[7] This statement implies that businesses and profits rightfully belong to workers, not business owners, and this belief stems from the labor theory of value.

The labor theory of value is the *core reason* socialists believe capitalism is evil and unjust and needs to be destroyed. Mick Brooks, writing for *In Defense of Marxism*, underscores the absolute significance of this theory when it comes to socialism:

> One of the basic ideas of Karl Marx that is constantly being denied by the bourgeois is his theory of value. This is understandable because from this very theory flow all the other conclusions of Marx, in particular that of the need to overthrow capitalism if we are to put to an end to all the contradictions of this unjust system which condemns millions of human beings to abject poverty, mass unemployment, periodic economic crises, and wars.[8]

The problem with the labor theory of value is it was completely debunked by economists in the late 1800s and universally replaced by the *subjective theory of value*.

Steven Horwitz, Professor of Enterprise at Ball State University, likens the labor theory of value to the old days when it was widely believed the earth was at the center of the universe and everything else in space revolved around the earth. Now we know in truth that the earth revolves around the sun and the old theory has been discarded.

Once widely accepted, the labor theory of value has been discarded by nearly all economists and replaced with the subjective theory of value. For some inexplicable reason, however, the labor theory still has a wide following in academic circles. Horwitz writes,

> Today, the labor theory of value has only a minuscule number of adherents among professional economists, but it remains all too common in other academic disciplines when they discuss economic issues, as well as among the general public.[9]

The *subjective* theory of value maintains that the price of a product or service is not inherent in the product. Humans, this theory recognizes, have the capability of imputing value *into* products and services. Humans can assign their own value based on their personal preferences and how useful they believe a product or service will be to them. They are able to say, "I am willing to pay more money for this blue chair than that green chair because I love the color blue!"—even though the two chairs are otherwise identical and took the same amount of materials and labor to produce.

For any God-fearing person, the subjective theory is intuitive. The Bible teaches that *human value* is not derived from our chemical makeup (we were formed out of dust! dust is worth nothing!) nor by our work or actions ("when we display our righteous deeds, they are nothing but filthy rags"…"you are more valuable to God than a whole flock of sparrows"…"He chose us in Him before the foundation of the world").[10] The Bible teaches that human beings are valuable because *God says we are valuable*. He has imputed value *into* us. We are so valuable in His eyes that He paid the highest possible price for us: the life of His own Son.

41

If God imputes value into His creation, it naturally follows that we human beings—created in His image—would also have the ability to impute value into the things around us.

It is possible, then, for a smart businessman to produce a product people believe they *really* want and need. He can create a product that they value highly...*more highly* than the cost of materials and labor it takes to produce it. Thus it is possible for him to justly and morally make a profit above and beyond the amount he pays his workers.

Horwitz writes,

Rather than seeing the value of outputs being determined by the value of the inputs like labor, the subjective theory of value showed that it's the other way around: *the value of inputs like labor were determined by the value of the outputs they helped to produce.*[11]

The subjective theory is vitally important to understand; because if it is true, it proves capitalism is not inherently an evil and oppressive system like socialists claim it is (although evil and oppression can occur, of course, through sinful people who exist within any and all systems).

Democratic Socialism

Socialists throughout history have always shared similar underlying beliefs and goals, but specific strategies for the implementation of these beliefs and goals vary from one group of socialists to another.

For example, Thomas DiLorenzo points out in *The Problem With Socialism* that socialists have learned over time that in order to gain control of an economy it is not necessary for the government to literally confiscate and oversee the everyday operations of all factories, major businesses, and farms like Chairman Mao did in China. Private businesses, other socialists realize, can still be allowed to exist under socialism *because a system of pervasive government regulation can be just as effective at controlling the economy as literal government ownership of the means of production.*[12]

The preferred flavor of socialism in our day is called "democratic socialism." The dictionary defines democratic socialism as "a political movement advocating a gradual and peaceful transition from capitalism to socialism by democratic means."[13]

Whereas the communist movements of last century called for an immediate and violent overthrow of capitalism; today's democratic socialism calls for a slow, gradual, and "peaceful" transition away from capitalism toward socialism.

Bernie Sanders, one of the most visible spokesmen and protagonists of democratic socialism in the United States at the time I am writing this book, explained democratic socialism for us in this way:

> I mean, to me, it means democracy, frankly. That's all it means. And we are living in an increasingly undemocratic society in which decisions are made by people who have huge sums of money. And that's the goal that we have to achieve.[14]

Let's unpack this. Democracy. What does he mean by that?

When democratic socialists use the word *democracy*, they are saying three things. First, they are saying they want a government system that is purely democratic in nature. Then they are highlighting two more key components of democratic socialism: collectivism and anti-totalitarianism.

Pure Democracy

Wait a second. Isn't the United States of America already democratic? Hasn't democracy always been a dearly-held American value? Aren't we already the world's *poster child* for democracy?! Is Bernie Sanders telling us our right to vote is slipping away from us?

When we hear the word "democracy," we Americans feel a certain surge of emotion. It gives us great pride to go to the ballot box and make our voices heard. Socialists' purposeful emphasis on this term has caused a lot of confusion due to America's deeply-held love of democracy. It is misleading.

We need to remember first and foremost that our government is not and never has been a *pure democracy*; it is a *republic*. A *democratic republic*. Socialists want to change our government from a *democratic republic* into a *pure democracy* and there is a vast difference between the two.

A democratic republic gives a voice to *all* people but also protects the people *from the people*. The electoral college and the Senate, for example, are "undemocratic." Having these certain "undemocratic" elements as part of our government acts as a check against the potential tyranny of the masses. It makes sure people in Wyoming have just as much a say as those living in New York and California and ensures that the entire country doesn't have to live the way New York and California tell us to live.

But socialists want to get rid of the Senate. They want to get rid of the electoral college. They want to remove all the built-in checks and balances intrinsic to our republic. They want a pure democracy.

Ancient Greek historian Polybius (200-118 B.C.) is famous for his studies on the balance of power and mixed constitution that made the Roman Republic (509-27 B.C.) a success. America's founding fathers were greatly influenced by his writings. In *Histories VI*, Polybius describes the natural progression of events that occurs when people turn their government into a pure democracy:

Thus the only hope still surviving unimpaired is in themselves, and to this they resort, making the state a democracy...

But when the new generation arises...they have become so accustomed to freedom and equality that they no longer value them, and begin to aim at pre-eminence...

Hence when by their foolish thirst for reputation they have created among the masses an appetite for gifts and the habit of receiving them, democracy in its turn is abolished and changes into a rule of force and violence. For the people, having grown accustomed to feed at the expense of others and to depend for their livelihood on the property of others...institute the rule of violence; and now uniting their forces massacre, banish, and plunder, until they degenerate again into perfect savages and find once more master and monarch.[15]

Polybius and our founding fathers realized what socialists today have forgotten: that unchecked democracy, with no built-in protection against human nature, inevitably leads to *mob rule, chaos, violence, and tyranny*.

Democratic Socialism is Collectivist

Democratic socialists also want to redefine what democracy is used for. The democracy for which the United States of America has traditionally been known is not the same sort of "democracy" democratic socialism espouses at all.

Democracy in the United States has historically stood for the right of citizens to vote for representatives who will serve in government on their behalf in order to promote and protect their sacred *individual* liberties.

To socialists, however, "democracy" means something altogether new for America. Democratic socialism's "democracy" is about the right of citizens to vote into place a government bureaucracy that will serve on their behalf as *collective* "owners" of the means of production!

To democratic socialists, democracy is about placing more and more economic decisions that have traditionally been made by individual consumers and producers (each and every one of us), via our own financial choices in the *free market*, into the hands of a democratically-appointed government bureaucracy.

And not just financial and business decisions—but also decisions about our personal lives.

The Democratic Socialists of America website explains, "Democratic socialists believe that both the economy and society should be run democratically—to meet public needs, not to make profits for a few."[16] This new kind of democracy is a complete upheaval and reversal of the democracy the United States has traditionally enjoyed.

This kind of democracy takes away the rights and liberties of the individual. It takes away the freedom to make our own choices about what we value most and where we want to spend our money, how much we are able and willing to spend on certain items, how much of our own capital we want to risk in business ventures, and even (as F.A. Hayek illustrated so well in *The Road to Serfdom*) our choice of employment,[17] in order to elevate rights of the *collective*—so that everyone can be materially "equal."

Democratic Socialism is (A Little Too) Loudly Anti-Totalitarian

To understand even further the democratic socialists' emphasis on the word "democracy," we must keep in mind the frightfully embarrassing legacy the term "socialism" carries with it. The violence, oppression, mass starvation, mass murder, and slave labor camps that emerged out of last century's socialist/

communist/fascist movements are quite a history for socialism to overcome.

We already talked in detail about the violence, suffering, and catastrophic results of last century's communist movement in China; but that was just one example of the death and destruction caused in the name of "socialism" in the 20th century. Russia had a very similar revolution story that ended in tens of millions of innocent deaths in the Soviet *Gulag*, or prison labor camp system. Some people in America today don't realize that the Nazi and Fascist movements in Germany and Italy were also *socialist movements* that emerged out of the same ideological underpinnings as Soviet Russia and Communist China. "Nazi" stands for *National Socialist German Workers' Party*.

In the 20th century, socialism was responsible for the greatest violence and gave rise to the harshest dictatorships the world has ever seen. This is an undeniable fact. In light of this, today's socialists must go to incredible lengths to establish that *their* version of socialism is different, separate, and superior to all socialist movements of the past.

When democratic socialists talk about *democracy* they are proclaiming very loudly that they are 100% against totalitarian rule. They are 100% against dictatorship. They are 100% against violence. They are 100% for peace. They are 100% for the people.

They are proclaiming, in effect, *This time it will turn out differently. This time we will finally get it right.*

But will they?

"We call ourselves socialists to remind everyone that we have a vision of a better world."

—DEMOCRATIC SOCIALISTS
OF AMERICA

4

DEMOCRATIC SOCIALISM DEFINED:

THE IDEAL

If there is still some fuzziness blurring your understanding of the meaning of democratic socialism, you are not alone. An argument could be made that the etherealness of socialism is in fact one of its fundamental components. It is certainly part of its allure. Alexander Solzhenitsyn, famous Soviet Gulag survivor, wrote in the 1970s,

> There is not even a precise definition of socialism that is generally recognized; all we have is a sort of hazy shimmering concept of something good, something noble, so that two socialists talking to each other about socialism might just as well be talking about completely different things...But socialism defies logic. You see, it is an emotional impulse, a kind of worldly religion, and nobody has the slightest need to study or even to read the teachings of its early prophets.[18]

The deeper we dig into the concept of socialism, the more we come to understand that it is much more than a certain set of political and economic policies. Socialism is also at its core a deeply held belief system.

It is an *ideal*.

∽o∾

To understand the socialist *ideal*, it's helpful at this point to look back at Karl Marx's original definition of the word "socialism." In Marxist theory, "socialism" is the bridge that carries a society away from capitalism toward "full communism."

"Full communism," to Marx, had a different meaning from the authoritarianism we associate today with the "communism" of countries like China, Cuba, and Venezuela; although "full communism" was undoubtedly what Mao was shooting for in the Chinese Cultural Revolution. "Full communism" is the Marxist term that describes the end goal of Marxism and the dream of socialists everywhere. It refers to a future "equal" society in which divisions between people are dissolved and social classes cease to exist.

To Marx, "full communism" was a beautiful utopia.

Although specific expectations of the socialist ideal fluctuate and change with the times—and although the word "utopia" is out of fashion these days—socialism is the human quest for *social justice* on earth. For some, utopia exists as a shining dream; for others, it is more of a "scientific" goal. But socialism maintains that humanity can and must, in its own power, attain a harmonious state of existence that is marked by both material and social equality and freedom from oppression. This is the socialist *ideal*.

An Age-Old Dream

There's a general feeling mounting in the United States today that democratic socialism is a new, up-and-coming movement. It's *progressive*. It's an evolutionary step *forward*. It's *modern*. It stands ready to propel us *ahead* into a future of greater equality and purer justice than humanity has ever known before.

Russian mathematician Igor Shafarevich disproves this idea completely. His monumental work *The Socialist Phenomenon* is a meticulous analysis of socialist societies visible throughout history. In this book, he takes the reader on a journey—not just back to Karl Marx and his contemporaries, but all the way back to the most ancient of civilizations. In the Introduction to his book, he opens with the following excerpts from a scene in one of Aristophanes' plays from Ancient Greece. It's so striking I want to include it here.

The first example takes us to Athens in 392 B.C. during the great urban Dionysia, when Aristophanes presented his comedy *Ecclesiazusae* or *The Congresswomen.* Here he depicts a teaching fashionable in the Athens of the time. The plot is as follows: The women of the city, wearing beards and dressed in men's clothing, come to the assembly and by a majority vote pass a resolution transferring all power in the state to women. They use this power to introduce a series of measures, which are expounded in a dialogue between Praxagora, the leader of the women, and her husband, Blepyros. Here are several quotations:

PRAXAGORA:
Compulsory Universal Community Property is what I propose to propose; across-the-board Economic Equality, to fill those fissures that scar our society's face. No more the division between Rich and Poor. ... We'll wear the same clothes, and share the same food. ... My initial move will be to communalize land, and money, and all other property, personal and real.

BLEPYROS:
But take the landless man who's invisibly wealthy... because he hides his silver and gold in his pockets. What about him?

PRAXAGORA:
He'll deposit it all in the Fund. ... I'll knock out walls and remodel the City into one big happy household, where all can come and go as they choose. ... I'm pooling the women, creating a public hoard for the use of every man who wishes to take them to bed and make babies.

BLEPYROS:
A system like this requires a pretty wise father to know his own children.

PRAXAGORA:
But why does he need to? Age is the new criterion: Children will henceforth trace their descent from all men who might have begot them. ...

BLEPYROS:
Who's going to work the land and produce the food?

PRAXAGORA:
The slaves. This leaves you just one civic function: When the shades of night draw on, slip sleekly down to dinner... The State's not going to stint. Its hand is full and open, its heart is large, it'll stuff its menfolk free of charge, then issue them torches when dinner's done and send them out to hunt for fun.[19]

Sound familiar? 2,400 hundred years ago we see the same blurring of gender identification and roles we see today. Women want to appear exactly the same as men; yet at the same time they want to gain control over men. There is also a clear emphasis on *democracy*...the women win by majority vote! We see a push for equality and equal distribution of wealth, as well as a belief that these policies will heal society's deepest problems.

We see free sex, the destruction of the family, the raising of children by adults besides their own parents, and a sweeping vision for peace and harmony. We also see a picture of a benevolent, fun-loving government that will provide plenty for everyone; ushering in ease, fulfillment, and enjoyment of life *(for everyone except the slaves, of course)*. We even have a call for open borders and a mention of walls!

In reading these words it becomes immediately evident that the socialist movement we see burgeoning in Western society today is not new or "progressive" (in the true sense of the word) at all. It is in fact *the same old red thread* which has woven itself, in one form or another and in varying degrees, into the stories of many societies in different parts of the world all throughout history.

Shafarevich identifies this thread running through the ancient societies of Mesopotamia, Egypt, and China; and finds it visible in societies such as the Incan Empire and the Jesuit State in Paraguay. He then follows the thread to Marx and more modern examples of socialism, including his own all too personal experience of socialism in the USSR. He writes,

> All such [socialist] doctrines have a common core—they are based on the complete rejection of the existing social structure. They call for its destruction and paint a picture of a more just and happy society in which the solution to all the fundamental problems of the times would be found.[20]

The Red Thread Defined

From his collection of historical data, Shafarevich finds four commonalities[21] that link all these various socialist movements together. These four pillars have been present in one form or another (and with varying degrees of success of implementation) in every socialist movement in the history of the world— including the communist and fascist movements of last century. They together comprise what I call the identifying "red thread" of socialism:

1. **The Abolition of Private Property**
   (either communality of property or state ownership/control/regulation of property)

2. **The Abolition of the Family**
   (de-emphasizing its role, weakening family ties, the abolition of certain functions of the family, separating children from their parents, free love, the communality of wives, women moved to work outside the home)

3. **The Abolition of Religion (especially Christianity)**
   (hostility toward religion, often hatred of the cross and the church)

4. **Communality or Equality**
   (*not* an of equality of rights under the law but material equality and the equalization of personalities or identity of behavior; ultimately the destruction of the individual)

Each of these four pillars is clearly evident in our culture today, indicating a strong and growing presence of socialism in the United States.

While no one is showing up on our doorsteps to confiscate businesses and force us to live in communes, **the abolition of private property** is occurring nonetheless through more understated means. The government is taking ownership of more and more of our privately owned wealth through the avenue of *taxation*. We also see increasing government control of land, businesses, and wealth through extensive government *regulation*. We are witnessing an alarming loss of *privacy* through technology that can watch and listen to us everywhere, including inside the "privacy" of our own homes. Recently-proposed COVID-19 tracking measures, if enacted, would take this loss of privacy to a whole new level. Society's accepting response to the destructive 2020 post-George Floyd riots stands as a clear indication that the basic human right to own and protect private property is disappearing quickly in America. Socialists are openly pushing for a redistribution of wealth.

The abolition of the family is just about complete. The traditional definition of a family has been tossed out and reconfigured...to the point where gender itself has become ambiguous. Many young people reject the idea of marriage altogether; single motherhood is a norm. A traditional family where mom and dad stay together for life has become rare. Stay-at-home moms and homemakers are even rarer: most women have been either forced by financial pressures or convinced by feminism that it is in their best interest to work outside the home. Most of our nation's young children are raised communally in daycares and educated in government-run public schools.

Tolerance has ushered in **the abolition of religion**. Today we are witnessing a major societal swing toward atheism and also toward the widespread belief that all religions are basically the same. Society rages against the idea of absolute Truth and rages against Jesus of the Bible who claims to be the Only Way to God. It is no secret that in this nation there has been a mass exodus of young people from Christian churches. Bible-believing Christians are now considered to be bigots. Tax exemption status for churches and religious organizations is threatened, and religious liberty is holding on by the tiniest of threads.

It seems that everyone these days is fighting for **equality.** Many people in this country do not realize that this is *a signature sign* of socialism. This is its mark; a calling card, so to speak. Social justice, white privilege, spreading the wealth...these "struggles" erupting in our society and confusing so many people are further evidence of a rising socialist revolution in the United States.

Shafarevich shows that each of the four hallmarks of socialism listed above emerges from one single, overarching goal of socialism, which is *to suppress individuality*.

Why? Why would socialism need so badly to suppress individuality? This question brings us right back to the moral tug of war between *collectivism* and *individualism* we mentioned briefly in the previous chapter.

The Socialist Ideal Is A Collectivist Ideal

The United States of America was founded upon the concept of individualism.

American individualism comes from the firm Judeo-Christian understanding that every human being is created uniquely in the image of God and therefore holds equal moral *worth* or *value*—regardless of gender, race, religion, intelligence, health, or any other variable.

"So God created man in his own image, in the image of God he created him; male and female he created them." (ESV)

"I praise you, for I am fearfully and wonderfully made. Wonderful are your works; my soul knows it very well." Psalm 139:14 (ESV)

"There is neither Jew nor Greek, there is neither slave nor free, there is no male and female, for you are all one in Christ Jesus." Galatians 3:28 (ESV)

The Bible teaches that each and every *individual* has a free will and that every *individual* is responsible before God and His Law for his or her own beliefs, actions, attitudes, and decisions: "For we must all stand before Christ to be judged. We will each receive whatever we deserve for the good or evil we have done in this earthly body." 2 Corinthians 5:10

Traditionally, the United States (with the deplorable and hypocritical exception of slavery based on race, which stood in stark contradiction to this principle) has existed to uphold the sovereign freedom of the individual. The personal liberties outlined in the Bill of Rights (the right to privacy, the right to freedom of speech, etc.) were put in place to protect the sanctity of the *individual*.

The economic system of capitalism honors the ideas of God-given equal *worth* of individuals and the *responsibility* and *right* those individual citizens have to freely make their own economic and personal decisions according to their unique values and preferences.

There is, however, increasingly heavy social and political pressure on Americans today to forsake individualism in favor of collectivism. We are being told that we should sacrifice and lay aside our individual liberties, diversity of beliefs, unique goals, and personal property for the sake of equity and the "greater good."

Socialism is collectivist by nature, and collectivism denies the moral worth of the individual. It always prioritizes the "group" over the individual. In collectivist estimation, the worth of an individual is not all-important; a human's value comes only from the individual's existence as part of a greater whole.

So, instead of recognizing *individual* responsibility and holding *individuals* accountable for their *own* actions before the law, collectivism recognizes and enforces *collective* responsibility. It views entire groups of people as being collectively guilty for problems within society.

This is why all white people are being told to apologize to all black people for being racists; and why reparations are being demanded today to atone for slavery that ended 155 years ago. Socialism does not view racism as an individual problem to be dealt with on an individual basis as it arises in individual human hearts; it holds all white people collectively responsible for the problem of racism against all black people. It also holds our entire American society today collectively responsible for the crimes of slavery which were committed by some of our predecessors long ago.

To the collectivist, this reckoning is called *social justice*; but to the individualist, this is *injustice* in its purest form because it violates the concept of individual responsibility.

In the realm of economics, what collectivism means is that the *labor power* of an individual—as well as the *rewards* of his labor (his paycheck and property)—do not belong exclusively to that individual. They are *not* to be used to achieve the unique individual values and goals of that laborer and his nuclear family. Instead, collectivism views the labor power and the rewards of a person's labor as belonging to *society as a whole* and are to be used to further the *collective values and goals* of that society.

This is the essence of the socialist ideal. Socialism envisions a collective society in which everyone is working—not to provide for themselves and for their families—but for the common good of society and to further the larger community's values and goals.

To the collectivist, this sounds like heaven on earth; but to the individualist, this is the very definition of *slavery*.

Equality and Social Justice Redefined

Equality and social justice are the proud and lofty words stirring our society into a frenzy today. What decent human being wouldn't want to stand up and fight for equality and justice?!

What many Americans don't realize is that these concepts are hallmarks of socialism and that the words are being used deceptively. Socialist "equality" and "social justice" mock the Judeo-Christian understanding of "equality" and "justice."

The words may look the same, but socialism gives them a completely new meaning.

Biblical equality maintains that every human, each being different and unique, has equal *worth* or *value* in the eyes of God. It rises from the understanding that God has one set, unmoving, and unchangeable measure of justice. *His righteous Laws are eternal.* His scale of justice never plays favorites; every individual is weighed by God on the same scale.

Our country was founded on the belief that every human being should also stand on equal footing before the Law of this Land. The U.S. Constitution and Bill of Rights would not make distinctions between rich and poor nor nobility and peasant. Its fixed measure of justice and the liberties it protected would extend equally to every citizen.

The goal of traditional American equality is *liberty*; that is, for individual rights of unique individuals to be equally protected by an unmoving Rule of Law. *This is true equality.*

Equality of Outcome

This does not mean, however, that everyone *turns out exactly the same* or *attains the same level of material prosperity;* and *this* is what socialists want. Socialist "equality" demands equality of outcome.

Socialists want the government to control all the moving economic and societal variables that can affect—positively or negatively—the results of a person's labor so everyone in society will end up with an equal amount of material wealth and possessions. Socialism uses the power and force of government to take money and possessions away from one person who has "more" in order to give it to another who has "less."

Law, under socialism, is no longer fixed. Socialist "equality" presumes to make arbitrary distinctions between individuals, treating different groups of people differently. There is one scale of justice and taxation for the rich and another for the poor.

The Bible calls for all followers of God to give generously to those in need; it calls for us to share our *own* wealth and possessions generously, sacrificially, and voluntarily. However, it never condones or permits taking *other people's* money away from them by force for any reason. This is called, in plain English terms, theft.

Socialist "equality" is a clear divergence from true equality and justice as defined by the Word of God. Socialist "equality" tips the scales of true justice and therefore results in gross *inequality*.

Equality of Identity

Socialist "equality" also denotes something more; it includes equality of *identity*. If the shining socialist ideal is for everyone to work happily together to achieve the same collective values and goals, it becomes necessary for everyone in society to become more and more "equal" to one another (that is, the same as one another) in thought, opinion, and behavior. We can't join together to live in harmony under socialism if we have warring ideals. Shafarevich explains,

> In socialist ideology…the understanding of equality is akin to that used in mathematics (when one speaks of equal numbers or equal triangles), i.e., this is in fact identity, the abolition of differences in behavior as well as in the inner world of the individuals constituting society.[22]

For socialism to work, peoples' differences have to be diminished. Expressions of uniqueness and individuality must be stifled as much as possible.

This is why we are being told in America today that there is no difference between men and women and why even the most basic human concept of gender is offensive. This is why ideologies that contradict Leftist agendas are being labeled "hate speech;" and why some big tech companies are beginning to censor and mark dissenting content as "dangerous." Our society is grasping for socialist *equality of identity*. The more we all look, sound, think, and act alike, the more fully the socialist ideal can be implemented.

In the end, socialist "equality" and "social justice" are counterfeits of true equality and true biblical justice. They promise an end to oppression, but in reality, they are masked thieves waiting to rob us of our liberty and strip us of our humanity.

Same Ideal, New Methodology

The communist movements of last century were aiming for the same collectivist ideal that the democratic socialist dreams of today. What separates democratic socialism from those movements is that it offers a new and improved *method* of reaching its ideal. Democratic socialism still calls for revolution; but instead of an outward, visible, violent revolution like we saw in China and the USSR, democratic socialism seeks to implement its revolution "peacefully"—that is, democratically.

You will remember that Merriam-Webster defines democratic socialism as "a political movement advocating a gradual and peaceful transition from capitalism to socialism by democratic means."[23]

That sounds positive, doesn't it? Peace! Democracy! Maybe the world is making some progress after all.

But how is such a revolution achieved?

How is it possible to change the mindset of millions of citizens in a modern, wealthy, thriving capitalist society to such an extent that they will happily and willingly vote socialism into place?

How is it possible to alter the way an entire society views reality?

There is only one answer:

Ideological subversion.

"Supreme excellence consists in breaking the enemy's resistance without fighting."

—SUN TZU, CHINESE MILITARY STRATEGIST, CIRC. 500 B.C

5

21ST CENTURY DEMOCRATIC SOCIALISM

REVOLUTION BY IDEOLOGICAL SUBVERSION

Fifty years ago, America was given a gift she ignored.

A steady trickle of survivors and defectors from oppressive communist countries like China and the USSR desperately fought their way to the freedom of our shores. They arrived battered, deeply shaken, and also spiritually awakened by all they had seen and experienced.

Our yawning indifference to their horror stories alarmed them. They were appalled that the United States kept sending money to and doing business with the Communists.

What shocked them, even more, was a growing realization, as they acclimated to life in the United States and began interacting with American culture, that the same cultural fissions and tremors which had arisen in their own countries 80 years prior were already clearly visible in the United States then in the 1970s and 80s. *The demons of socialism were already watering their seeds of destruction in America back then.*

These men and women, wizened from their intimacy with deep suffering, tried to shake us awake. They tried to tell us about the lies they and their countrymen had believed; and about the pure, unadulterated evil they had witnessed and experienced as a result. The pain. The hatred. The disillusionment. The enslavement. The millions of innocent lives slaughtered in the name of "progress" and "social justice."

Some of these courageous survivors dedicated the rest of their lives to warning us about the evils they saw threatening the West—despite the fact that we didn't listen. Alexander Solzhenitsyn, communist-turned-Christian and survivor of the Gulag, was one of these men. I grew up in Southern Vermont in the 1980's unaware that this remarkable man and his family were hiding from Soviet authorities in a small Vermont town only 60 miles from my childhood home. He was there all my growing up years: fervently, desperately writing. Compelled to chronicle the evils he and his countrymen had experienced in the USSR, he wrote them down and begged the world to learn from Russia's catastrophic mistakes.

Solzhenitsyn viewed socialism as the manifestation of an epic, worldwide tide of evil sweeping the world. It had first risen its ugly head in Russia; but, he believed, it would never be content to stop there.

In 1975 he wrote,

> From 1917 to 1959 socialism cost the Soviet Union 110 million lives! When there is a geological upheaval, continents do not topple into the sea immediately. The first thing that happens is that the fatal initial crevasse must appear someplace. For a variety of reasons it so happened that this crevasse first opened up in Russia, but it might just as well have been anywhere else…

> It is with a strange feeling that those of us who come from the Soviet Union look upon the West of today. It is as though we were neither neighbors on the same planet nor contemporaries. And yet we contemplate the West from what will be your future, or we look back seventy years to

see our past suddenly repeating itself today. And what we see is always the same as it was then: adults deferring to the opinion of their children; the younger generation carried away by shallow, worthless ideas; professors scared of being unfashionable; journalists refusing to take responsibility for the words they squander to easily; universal sympathy for revolutionary extremists; people with serious objections unable or unwilling to voice them; the majority passively obsessed by a feeling of doom; feeble governments; societies whose defensive reactions have become paralyzed; spiritual confusion leading to political upheaval. What will happen as a result of all this lies ahead of us. But the time is near, and from bitter memory we can easily predict what these events will be.[24]

Yuri Bezmenov, an ex-KGB agent and Soviet defector, sounded a similar alarm to the West in the 1980s. From his own experience, he was able to provide a fascinating window into the inner workings of the KGB at that time. He estimated that a whopping 85% of the KGB's resources were dedicated to the task of spreading communist ideas to other societies—with the clear aim of destroying these existing societies—and that they were doing this through *subversion.*[25]

Bezmenov explained in his lectures that the communist tactics of *ideological subversion* were formulated upon the theories of an ancient Chinese general and military strategist named Sun Tzu who served China's military in the late Zhou Dynasty, roughly 500 B.C.[26] Sun Tzu is the presumed author of a classic work on military strategy titled *The Art of War.* The premise of his book is that "all war is deceit." He believed the highest art of war is not perfecting the use of physical weapons and military force, but destroying one's enemy without ever having to raise arms.

"The greatest victory is that which requires no battle. ... Engage people with what they expect; it is what they are able to discern and confirms their projections. It settles them into predictable patterns of response, occupying their minds while you wait for the extraordinary moment—that which they cannot anticipate."[27]

This book is a highly acclaimed classic, but to me, it reads like C.S. Lewis' *Screwtape Letters*. It is nothing less than a treatise on mastering the art of deception: *mastering the art of the lie*.

It is this philosophy that laid the framework for the KGB's communist war strategy of ideological subversion, and it is this philosophy, we are about to see, that is driving America's "peaceful" democratic socialist revolution today.

Ideological Subversion

Ideological subversion, also known as *psychological warfare*, is the process of defeating and destroying a nation without firing a shot. The American response to the COVID-19 crisis would be a supreme example of how this plays out in the end. It is astounding how quickly we laid down, rolled over, and handed over our economy and liberties for the sake of fear.

Bezmenov defined ideological subversion in this way:

> To change the perception of reality of every American to such an extent that despite the abundance of information, no one is able to come to sensible conclusions in the interest of defending themselves, their families, their community, and their country. It's a great brainwashing process which goes very slow.[28]

In his 1980s lectures, Bezmenov explained that communist subversion tactics were already operating full tilt in the United States at that time and with astonishing success. But it wasn't primarily Soviet agents instigating the bulk of this subversion, he noted with great surprise; it was Americans themselves doing it to other Americans! He believed this was "due to lack of moral standards."[29]

America, so it seemed, was hell-bent on destroying *herself*.

Understanding this concept of subversion is paramount if we wish to grasp what democratic socialism really is and how it works. Bezmenov explained that communist ideological subversion occurs in four stages: *demoralization, destabilization, crisis,* and *normalization.*

Stage 1: Demoralization

During this first stage, which typically takes 15-20 years to complete (this is the time it takes to fully educate one generation), Marxist ideology is intentionally and strategically pumped into society, beginning with students at every level of the education system.

Next, in order to make society at large more open to new ideas, subverters seek ways to exploit any weaknesses and cracks already present in the pillars of that society's culture. For example, anti-religious groups are encouraged and given a microphone. Other sub-culture, activist, and minority groups are put on a platform. Traditional family life is attacked (mothers are encouraged to work outside of the home, free love is celebrated, the definitions of marriage and family—not to mention gender—are challenged and changed, dependence on daycare is promoted, etc., etc.) Traditional forms of social life are also slowly replaced with fake alternatives (labor groups, community organizing groups, social media); and doubts are planted in people's minds regarding authority. Unhealthy habits such as eating junk food and using drugs are also encouraged... anything that will deaden people's defenses. Finally, media is transformed into a machine of propaganda that increasingly works to feed socialist ideas to the public.

Eventually, when this stage is complete,

Exposure to true information does not matter anymore. A person who is demoralized is unable to assess true information; the facts tell nothing to him. Even if I shower him with information...with authentic proof, with documents, with pictures...Even if I take him by force to the Soviet Union and show him [a] concentration camp, he will refuse to believe it...until he is going to receive a kick in his fat bottom. When the military boot crushes him, then he will understand; but not before that.[30]

Stage 2: Destabilization

During this next stage of subversion, which typically takes just 2-5 years, socialist ideas are taken one step further. They are injected not only into society at large but into the economy and the country's foreign relations and defense systems.

Leftist activists such as professors, student groups, and civil rights defenders are all instrumental in the process of destabilization. They are utilized for their passion. But, Bezmenov warned, when their usefulness in the subversive revolution runs out they inevitably find themselves kicked to the curb. These socialists activists always think they will be the ones who come to power—but they never do. They suffer the consequences of socialism right along with everyone else.

Stage 3: Crisis

Once a nation has been demoralized and destabilized, things can snowball very quickly into a point of crisis where normal systems of society are no longer able to function as such. Government, social structure, the economy—they all begin to collapse. Citizens by this point are exhausted and scared; desperate to return to some semblance of order. They begin looking for a strong leader—someone to rescue them.

Crisis, Bezmenov explains, always leads to one of two things: civil war (socialism steps up from the inside) or foreign invasion (socialism steps in from the outside).

Crisis is the moment for which subverters—after patiently working for decades—wait patiently. Once crisis has been reached, the battle is essentially over. It becomes very easy at this point for socialists to present themselves as the savior of society and to be cheered into power.

Stage 4: Normalization

In this final stage, the society welcomes socialism with open arms—she hails socialism as her savior. Socialists of course gladly step in to save the day. A new government is set up, and to maintain control, it becomes immediately necessary to stabilize the nation under the new system.

This, according to Bezmenov, is when the lie of socialism strips off her rainbow mask and exposes her true gruesome hues. Once socialism is finally put into place, order has to be restored for socialists to maintain control.

A great host of activists, agitators, and idealists—who throughout the revolution have been encouraged to make as much noise and wreak as much havoc within society as possible—now have to be silenced.

Government leaders, in this normalization phase, not only completely squelch all capitalist voices of opposition (in the past it has done this by whatever means necessary…threats, reeducation classes and camps, imprisonment, death); but they also in the end inevitably turn on their own supporters, their own socialist idealists. The truth is they don't need them anymore. Socialist leaders use their idealists as revolutionary stepstools to power and now easily discard them to maintain order and control.

Socialism is not loving; it's hideous and cruel. In the end, is not actually about social justice. It could care less about equality. It has no compassion for the plight of minorities and women. It is not interested in saving the environment. It is not concerned with erasing poverty. It does not love the LGBTQ community.

All of that is a lie.

It is in the normalization stage that socialist idealists wake up to the fact that they have been deceived by a lie that holds disastrous consequences.

In the end, socialism's true colors always come to light. Socialism is all and only about one thing: power. In the end, it is about the few gaining control over the many. All the rest—all its promises, all its claims, all its ideals—are indeed bands of a rainbow that vanish into the mist as quickly as they appeared.

Back in the 1980s, when Bezmenov was giving his lectures, he was shocked at the extent to which the first stage of ideological subversion (demoralization) was already complete in the United States.

It seems that his analysis was correct. As I type these words in 2020, the process of demoralization has long since been complete. America has been teetering through the destabilization phase for several years and now I believe the COVID-19 virus has catapulted us straight into crisis.

We are grasping for a savior, are we not? Someone or something to get us out of this mess. The government is all too willing to assume that position for us, and we are allowing it to take more and more control.

Washington is spinning its wheels and can't seem to get anything done, but keeps making promise after promise to bail us all out. The media has morphed into a propaganda-spewing monster. Experts tell us the economy, propped up today by the Federal Reserve, could collapse at any moment. China and other nations own more and more of our debt. Wallstreet is out of control. Our country is divided. Society is ripping apart at the seams.

Socialists are raising their voices louder and louder. They are standing up to get in line. They are claiming they can save us and gaining support in shocking numbers. Just listen to any of the recent Democratic debates—what was only recently considered extreme is now being touted as "centrist." The Republican Party also is aligning itself more with socialist ideals. We don't need Bernie Sanders to step into the White House for socialism to eat us alive. Its lies and policies are coming at us from every direction imaginable.

Democratic socialism is generally accepted as a more moderate, "less dangerous" form of socialism than communism; but that is a gross miscalculation. Twentieth-century communism implemented its destructive socialist policies openly, violently and forcefully. Twenty-first century democratic socialism is doing so slowly, patiently, and subversively.

We must understand that as time marches on, Evil is not backing off or letting up on its game; *it is ramping it up*. Democratic socialism is not a *moderate* form of socialism; it is an *advanced* form of socialism. It is an implementation of the "highest art of war."

It is a master class deception.

Because of its deeply subversive nature, democratic socialism may—in the end—prove to be the deadliest and most destructive form of socialism the world has ever seen.

"Socialism means slavery."

—LORD JOHN ACTON

6

WHERE ARE WE HEADED?

OPPRESSION

We don't need to be prophets to see the writing on the wall for America; all we need to do is take an honest look around us. The United States is walking deeper and deeper into a trap of financial oppression, we are slowly allowing our liberties to be stripped away from us, and we are placing ourselves in grave and immediate danger of tyranny.

Financial Oppression

For decades America has been injecting socialist economic policies into its economy, and we are beginning to feel the harsh repercussions of this today.

In our inner cities, "sharing the wealth" through Welfare programs has not lifted citizens out of poverty as we hoped; it has trapped them more deeply inside it, causing deep hardships. More and more homeless people are dwelling in tents alongside our streets.

For the middle class, the tax burden is heavy and grows heavier every year. The more a person makes, the more the government confiscates in taxes, and already in America today it often pays to make less. You don't have to be an expert in economics to realize that this kind of economic demotivation is not good for society.

Even before COVID-19 came on the scene, small businesses everywhere were fighting to stay afloat. Excessive regulations have closed the doors of small businesses and farms from coast to coast; new, innovative companies have trouble making it off the ground. Government regulations keep mounting, and it simply costs too much—in time, money, and headaches—to keep up. More and more we are discovering that only the large, *government-subsidized* enterprises can compete. Government intervention created the monopolies that are crushing our small businesses.

We are also experiencing a nationwide epidemic of massive personal indebtedness, which has been encouraged by the socialist practice of creating artificially low interest rates. People who cannot afford loans have been swindled into believing they can; now they are strapped with debt. College-educated adults who should be kickstarting their careers are stuck working at coffee shops and grocery stores with little hope of ever escaping the mountain of debt on their shoulders.

Socialists blame capitalism for the financial pressures American citizens are facing today, but these problems are not the result of capitalism at all. They are the direct result of the socialist policies which have gradually over time been mixed into our "free market" economy. These attempts by our government to regulate the market—or control it—are handicapping it.

The free market economy cannot work properly when it is not free. F.A. Hayek writes in *The Road to Serfdom*,

> ...the universal struggle against competition promises to produce...something in many respects even worse, a state of affairs which can satisfy neither planners nor liberals [in the classic sense of the word; i.e. proponents of the free market]: a sort of syndicalist or "corporative" organization of industry,

in which competition is more or less suppressed but planning is left in the hands of the independent monopolies of the separate industries.[31]

This describes the situation in which the United States presently finds itself. Monopolies hold far too much power over the market, and the United States' economy is in a bind. Socialism has brought us here.

Our nation is already far more saturated with socialism than we realize. Just how socialist are we? The answer to this question is perhaps difficult to gauge, but measuring our present economy against Karl Marx's Ten Planks of Communism sheds some startling insight.

Back in 1848 Marx and Engels, in *The Communist Manifesto*, listed the ten steps (or "planks") necessary to *destroy* a capitalist free-market economic system and to *replace* it with the economic foundations necessary for communism.

An argument can be made that traces of all ten of these planks can be seen in our economic system today. Eight of the ten are immediately evident, so let's take a look at them here:[32]

Communist Plank #1:
Abolition of private property in land and application of all rents of land to public purpose.

While American citizens still appear to have the right to own private property, what we can do on and with "our" property is not really up to us, is it? How we use our land is tightly controlled by the Bureau of Land Management and through zoning laws, environmental regulations, etc. Homeowners are also burdened by perpetual property taxes, which continuously siphon away wealth and are an indication that we *don't actually own* our property. Property taxes are theft.

Communist Plank #2:
A heavy progressive or graduated income tax.

The progressive income tax was first imposed upon U.S. citizens in 1913 and has been present ever since. Leftists want to continue to raise taxes across the board and also increase the slant of tax graduation.

Communist Plank #3:
Abolition of all rights of inheritance.

In our nation, this is occurring backhandedly through taxes. If, after all the taxes we have to pay throughout our lifetime, we manage to make it to our deathbed with anything left to pass on to our children, the "death tax" ensures that very little to nothing will be left in the end for our beneficiaries. For white Americans to have the ability to leave an inheritance to their children is increasingly being portrayed as unjust and the result of white-on-black oppression.[33]

Communist Plank #5:
Centralization of credit in the hands of the state, by means of a national bank with State capital and an exclusive monopoly.

The Federal Reserve Board was instituted in 1913 as well. It can print currency at will and regulates the activities of all U.S. banks. It controls almost all other aspects of the American financial market as well. Our banks and financial systems, though "privately-owned" on paper, are almost completely controlled by the regulation of The Fed.

Communist Plank #6:
Centralization of the means of communications and transportation in the hands of the State.

The Department of Transportation and Federal Communications Commission have been established to regulate and subsidize these "privately-owned" means.

Communist Plank #7:
Extension of factories and instruments of production owned by the state, the bringing into cultivation of waste lands, and the improvement of the soil generally in accordance with a common plan.

Once again, the government does not "own" all these lands and means of production, but it effectively controls them via regulation through the Department of Agriculture, Department of Commerce and Labor, Department of Interior, the Environmental Protection Agency, Bureau of Land Management, Bureau of Reclamation, Bureau of Mines, National Park Service, and the IRS.

Communist Plank #8:
Equal liability of all to labor. Establishment of industrial armies, especially for agriculture.

The socialist ideology of "equality" ("sameness")—as well as rising costs of living due to inflation and the activities of The Fed—have already effectively moved almost all American women into the workforce. The Social Security Administration and The Department of Labor further encourage equal liability of all to labor and, of course, impose regulations on labor.

Communist Plank #10:
Free education for all children in public schools. Abolition of children's factory labor in its present form. Combination of education with industrial production.

Today we are so accustomed to the idea of "free" [taxpayer funded] public education that we can't imagine any other alternative. In the early days of the United States, however, things were different. Parents were the ones in control of the education of their children, not the government. They had a say and a role in determining what and how their children were taught—and America was not a nation of illiterate citizens. It wasn't until progressivism began gaining popularity in the late 19th century that more and more states began to implement compulsory education laws, transferring control of children's education away from parents into the hands of the government. By 1917 every U.S. state had compulsory education laws. Today many people feel they have no choice but to entrust their children to their local government-run public school. In most parts of America, only the wealthy can easily afford school "choice," and some states are increasing homeschool regulations, making that option more difficult.

At least eight of Marx's ten planks of communism have, in the updated democratic socialist form of regulatory control, already been implemented in the United States. These policies and bureaucracies are intended to work *against* competition in the free market economic system. They are meant to *cripple* capitalism, to *destroy* it, and to establish in its place a framework for socialism. Some of these policies have been working against our free market for over 100 years.

Continuing to raise the minimum wage, initiating more price controls (affordable prescription drugs, affordable healthcare, free college), establishing universal pre-K, increasing environmental regulation across the board, *giving out stimulus checks to every American in a national virus pandemic*…these are all further implementations of socialism poised to finish off the free market.

The more socialist policies we implement, the more the government will be involved in every aspect of our lives, and the less say we will have over what is "ours." The more socialist policies we implement, the more of the rewards of our labor will be stolen away from individual Americans and their families.

Today in America we are becoming the economic slaves of our government.

Loss of Liberty

Financial oppression is not the only form of slavery into which socialism ushers a society.

The sharp rise in public support for collective rights over individual rights means that all the precious liberties Americans have traditionally held are being attacked and undermined. They are slowly slipping away from us. *Freedom of speech, freedom of the press, freedom of religion, the right to bear arms, the right to own private property.*

We have all now experienced a taste of the heaviness that comes from having our normal freedoms curtailed during 2020's COVID-19 lockdowns. Unfortunately what we have already felt is just the beginning. It is only the tip of the iceberg if we continue to embrace socialism. More and more we will feel a tangible heaviness of oppression weighing down on us in place of the light and clear air of liberty.

One day we will wake up and realize we have traded our precious liberties for illusions and chains.

Tyranny

Although democratic socialism is, according to its stated ideals, outspokenly and vehemently against totalitarianism; its methodology paradoxically opens the door wide for tyranny to enter in.

Again and again, in socialist movements throughout history, there has surfaced an alarming disparity in nature between the *ideals* socialism claims to uphold and the *methods* it uses in an attempt to reach them. Mao preached that the Communist movement in China was *for* the people; yet again and again he turned on and trampled the people—even his fellow party members—in his attempt to implement the socialist ideal.

Hayek writes,

I have never accused the socialist parties of deliberately aiming at a totalitarian regime or even suspected that the leaders of the old school movements might ever show such inclinations. What I have argued…is that the unforeseen but inevitable consequences of socialist planning create a state of affairs in which, if the policy is to be pursued, totalitarian forces will get the upper hand. I explicitly stress that "socialism can be put into practice only by methods of which most socialists disapprove."[34]

The inescapable reality of socialism is that it actually, by its very definition, requires dictatorship.

Everyone working together in harmony and equity to reach one united goal for the good of humanity may sound like a grand and noble quest; but on the road to utopia socialists inevitably run into a glaring problem: *What do you do about all the individuals whose values fail to fall in line with the chosen "universal goal"?*

How do you handle counter-revolutionaries—which exist in all societies? What do you do with the capitalists who disagree with the methods of socialism? What do you do with the religious people who disagree with the premises of socialism? What do you do about the socialists who disagree with the decisions made by other socialists?!

All individuals who stand in opposition to socialism must at some point be bullied, silenced, and forced into compliance (repression), or they must be locked up (injustice), or they must be eliminated (genocide).

Shafarevich writes,

In pursuing this method we shall be astonished to discover that socialism…turns out to be a glaring contradiction. Proceeding from a critique of a given society, accusing it of injustice, inequality and lack of freedom, socialism proclaims—in the systems where it is expressed with the greatest consistency—a far greater injustice, inequality and slavery![35]

You will remember that Karl Marx originally described "socialism" as the transitionary *bridge between capitalism and true communism*; and that "true communism" refers to one version or another of "utopia"—the happy, harmonious society where everyone is working together for the common good.

Marx understood well that on the road to utopia there would be, at every turn, the problem of counter-revolutionaries who would rise in opposition to the movement. He, therefore, referred to socialism—this transitionary bridge between capitalism and true communism—as the "dictatorship of the proletariat."

He presented this period of dictatorship (a dictatorship of the oppressed class) as a sort of necessary evil that would have to exist temporarily so that humanity could reach its destiny. During this transitionary time, opposition to socialism would need to be continuously monitored and systematically stamped out *until there ceased to be any more opposition.*

Marx was teaching that on the road to utopia *the end justifies the means.* Humanity, socialism believes, must reach its destiny *by any means necessary.* Tragically this line of thinking has led straight to the torture, imprisonment, and murder of millions upon millions of innocent people around the globe.

It has not once led to anything even remotely resembling utopia.

Democratic Socialism and Fascism

The label "Nazi" is being thrown around a lot these days by Leftists in the United States. It's all the rage to compare President Trump with Adolf Hitler. People are truly afraid we're on the brink of totalitarian rule.

We *are* in danger of totalitarian rule. We are in immediate and grave danger of following right in Nazi Germany's footsteps. But the danger does not stem from President Trump.

Today our president's power and our government's power is still held in check (though more and more tenuously every moment...the House and Senate have been dismembering checks and balances for years!) by our Rule of Law protecting individual rights: our Constitution.

Limiting the power of government through checks and balances and binding it to a written Rule of Law acknowledges the simple fact that we humans are prone to corruption. It demonstrates the willingness of a society of people to be held accountable to a Higher Law than any law they themselves may wish to create at will.

Socialism, however, calls for the tearing down of our Constitution. It flagrantly denies the Judeo-Christian principle of the existence of an enduring Higher Law. It bristles against the idea of submitting to an unchangeable, unalterable, supreme Law designed to hold the force of government at bay and to protect the God-given rights of the *individual*.

National correspondent Ryan Cooper wrote an article for *The Week* entitled "The American Constitution is terrible. Let's throw it out and start over." He says,

> The American Constitution is an outdated, malfunctioning piece of junk—and it's only getting worse...The truth seems clear: America is going to have to overhaul its basic structure of government, or eventually it will fall to pieces.[36]

This opinion is prevalent among Leftists today, and as liberty-loving citizens of the United States, it is this train of thought we must fear. The Constitution—our Rule of Law that stands taller than any branch of government and higher than the changing tides of opinion, and which protects our individual liberties and limits the coercive power of government—is the only thing standing between us and tyranny.

Adolf Hitler didn't just decide one day to take over Germany. His rise to power was preceded by years and years of a swelling tide of socialist thought which:

1. influenced the thinking of the masses to a point where they were unable to correctly discern right from wrong;

2. slowly and deliberately dismembered Germany's Rule of Law; and

3. led to so much economic and political instability that the people were desperate for a strong leader to step in and rescue them.

It was in 1848 that Germans Marx and Engels first published *The Communist Manifesto.* By the early 1930s, when Hitler arrived on the scene, Germany—influenced heavily by these thinkers—had implemented socialist policies to such an extent that it was but a seamless, easy, natural step for Hitler to take control of the government. Hayek writes,

> It is important to point out once more in this connection that this process of the decline of the Rule of Law had been going on steadily in Germany for some time before Hitler came into power and that a policy well advanced toward totalitarian planning had already done a great deal of the work which Hitler completed...

> To say that in a planned society the Rule of Law cannot hold is, therefore, not to say that the actions of government will not be legal or that such a society will necessarily be lawless. It means only that the use of the government's coercive powers

will no longer be limited and determined by pre-established rules...By giving the government unlimited powers, the most arbitrary rule can be made legal; and in this way a democracy may set up the most complete despotism imaginable...[37]

The socialist ideology undergirding the democratic socialist movement in the United States today is the very same ideology that *originated* in Germany prior to the rise of Hitler and paved the way for the Nazis!

In fact, as Thomas DiLorenzo points out in *The Problem With Socialism*, today's democratic socialism is very similar to German and Italian socialist *fascism* because instead of taking literal ownership of all the means of production, as the communists did, it allows private ownership of businesses to continue to exist—but for the benefit of the government, not the individual.[38] Fascism, just like democratic socialism, was all about leveraging the power of government *regulation* to control people and the economy.

Hayek also says, speaking of the West—and specifically of Great Britain and the United States,

> At least some of the [socialist] forces which...destroyed freedom in Germany are also at work here and...the character and the source of this danger are, if possible, even less understood here than they were in Germany. The supreme tragedy is still not seen that in Germany it was largely people of good will, men who were admired and held up as models in the democratic countries, who prepared the way for, if they did not actually create, the forces which now stand for everything they detest...
>
> Few are ready to recognize that the rise of fascism and naziism was not a reaction against the socialist trends of the preceding period but a necessary outcome of these tendencies...As a result, many who think they themselves

infinitely superior to the aberrations of naziism, and sincerely hate all its manifestations, work at the same time for ideals whose realization would lead straight to the abhorred enemy.[39]

America, it's time to begin wrapping our minds around this. Socialism is not the glowing benefactor of social justice it claims to be. It is leading us straight toward Nazi Germany. It is leading us straight toward severe oppression.

"He sees that he must follow the counsel of the wise spirit, the dread spirit of death and destruction, and therefore accept lying and deception, and lead men consciously to death and destruction, and yet deceive them all the way so that they may not notice where they are being led."

—FYODOR DOSTOYEVSKY,
THE BROTHERS KARAMAZOV

7

SOCIALISM'S INTIMATE BEDFELLOW

DEATH

Socialism stands as the single greatest man-made cause of death in the history of the world.[40] It is an irrefutable fact that there is a haunting connection between socialism and human death—both figurative and literal death.

Figurative Death

Socialism's self-effort to rid the world of evil, reach humanity's full potential, improve quality of life for everyone, and reach social equity somehow actually manages to suck all the beauty, creativity, and diversity—the very *life!*—out of life.

It stifles personality and giftedness.

It leads to the death of liberty and justice. The death of ingenuity and choice. The death of prosperity, religion, and culture.

This is the tragic end of the pursuit of socialism's twisted, faulty version of "equality;" and what occurs when the rights of the "collective" are allowed to trump those of the individual. To build its utopia, socialism must take an entire society of living stones—unique, valuable, vibrant, individual human beings created in the image of God—and transform them into a massive pile of identical, manmade, human bricks.

Socialism forces everyone into one mold. What it desires is harmony, but what it produces is an excruciating, oppressive *sameness*. Life under socialism is never a shimmering utopia; life under socialism is deathly monotone. Socialist "equality" is an "equality" where everyone thinks the same implanted thoughts, speaks the same robotic mantras, and dreams the same blank dreams.

I witnessed this firsthand in China in 2007 when I tried in vain to ignite a spark of creativity in my English students. To my sorrow, I encountered within them no inner drive and no original dreams. The papers they wrote for me all sounded the same. Their dreams for the future consisted of landing whatever government job they could so they and their families could live a life of security.

Socialist "equality" is not beautiful; it is ghastly.

It crushes human souls.

Literal Death

Socialism does not end only in figurative death, however; it also leads to the literal death of human beings.

On a massive scale.

The alarming and grotesque reality we see in history is that the attempted implementation of socialism's twisted ideals has again and again produced a literal and staggering loss of human life.

This is not an exaggeration.

When we count up the numbers, as European scholars did in *The Black Book of Communism*, we find that in the 20th century the lie of socialism caused the deaths of over 100 million human beings.[41] (Solzhenitsyn would say that is a conservative number, estimating 110 million deaths in the Soviet Union alone.[42])

How did socialists accomplish such a feat? The pied piper Socialism dances its unsuspecting victims toward death down a myriad of different avenues. Sometimes death arrives as a result of failed economic policies; sometimes human death is simply deemed a necessary, calculated cost of reaching the socialist ideal.

Failed Economic Policies

Socialist economic policies have a proven track record of delivering exactly the opposite of what they promise. Instead of solving problems like poverty and hunger, socialist policies make them unimaginably worse.

Millions of Chinese peasants, working in farm communes, literally starved to death after being forced to send all their crops to the cities to feed their comrades there. Mao's impossibly high demands of the peasants led to devastating farming practices that created a man-made, widespread famine.

Stalin's economic programs also resulted in severe food shortages in the Soviet Union. As many as *nine million* Soviet peasants (mostly Ukrainian) died in the man-made famine of 1932-33 alone. Stalin let them die and in fact aided their death in an effort to crush the peasant resistance to his collectivization programs.

Thousands to millions of innocent civilians died as a result of the nuclear disaster of Chernobyl which occurred as a direct result of the communists trying to cover up how badly their policies had failed and to what dire financial straits the country had been pushed.

In more recent history, the once-wealthy nation of Venezuela has been reduced to severe food shortages and starvation as a direct result of its socialist policies.

In Canada, Norway, and Sweden...the supposed poster children of democratic socialism today...people with serious medical conditions are forced to wait months (sometimes fatally[43]) for medical treatment due to the inefficiency of their single-payer healthcare systems.

Cuba. Nicaragua. Ethiopia. Burma. Laos. Somalia. Yemen. The list of countries in which the failed economics of socialism has ended up harming humanity goes on and on.

Utopian Dreams Gone Awry

Socialism is linked with genocide as well.

The lie of the socialist ideal allows socialists to twist reality to such an extent that killing masses of innocent people appears in the moment to be the right, noble, and just thing to do. Again and again on the road to utopia, killing has been accepted as a perhaps unpleasant, but necessary key to ridding the world of oppression and reaching humanity's full potential.

When German citizens aided the Nazis in rounding up the Jews, *they believed they were doing their moral and civic duty to free the world from the evils of capitalism and improve the future of humanity.*

When young Chinese students tortured and killed elders in their villages who did not support the teachings of the Communist Party, *they believed they were taking a necessary stand against injustice and freeing the exploited class from poverty.*

When Soviet citizens turned in their neighbors to be sent to Siberian labor camps, never to be seen again, *they believed this action would lead to equality and a better future for their children.*

It may seem unimaginable today, as we sip our lattes while browsing the aisles of Target; but we will taste more senseless, hideous death in America if socialism continues to rise unchecked. We are gravely underestimating the magnitude of danger looming ahead.

I say "more death" because mass murder is already occurring in this nation—right under our very noses. We, the citizens of the United States of America, already have blood dripping from our hands.

We are already swimming in rivers of blood.

Today when we send our young women to abortion clinics in America, *we say we are standing on the side of compassion. We say we are liberating women from male domination and fighting for basic human rights.*

It turns out that democratic socialism is not less violent or bloodthirsty than communism; *it is just better at concealing its victims.*

Death in This House

In this country over one million babies are murdered every single year under the flag of "women's rights."

Since Roe v. Wade in 1973, it is estimated that more than 60 million unborn children have been eliminated in the United States of America.

The total number of Jews murdered by the Nazis is estimated at 6 million.[44] The estimated total of all the communist crimes of last century put together, as we noted, is 100 million. How dare we Americans living today point a self-righteous finger at anyone else in history?! If evil can be measured in numbers of human deaths, has there ever existed a more evil generation than ours in the history of the world?

Sixty million human lives is an unimaginably high number. It is an impossible number for our brains to comprehend. Stop for a moment and visualize the streets of New York City, with its teems and teems of busy people.

If you combine the current total populations of the United States' ten most populated cities—New York, Los Angeles, Chicago, Houston, Phoenix, Philadelphia, San Antonio, San Diego, Dallas, and San Jose—you have a total of 25.7 million people.

If you *double* that number, taking take *two* of each of the populations of the ten largest cities in America, you come to 51.4 million people.

We still haven't reached the total number of human beings we have "eliminated" in America since 1973. You would have to add the entire population of New York City a third time to get close.

We have annihilated the equivalent of every single person in New York, Los Angeles, Chicago, Houston, Phoenix, Philadelphia, San Antonio, San Diego, Dallas, and San Jose... *twice*. Then, as if that wasn't enough human blood, we went back and decimated the equivalent of the entire population of New York City a third time.

This, America, is what *our society* has done.

We have to stop here and feel the sickness and the horror, the crushing weight of this unimaginable crime we are committing against humanity.

It should make us ill. It should cause our knees to buckle.

Senseless death isn't something looming far ahead in our future; it is already happening right here inside our own house. The present-day reality of legalized abortion in the United States stands before us as a staggering, incriminating example of how the attempted implementation of the socialist ideal inevitably results in literal human death.

I do understand that a majority of Americans today, despite overwhelming moral and scientific evidence to the contrary, persist in viewing unborn children as sub-human; and do not, therefore, equate abortion with human death. It will serve us well here to remember that *Nazis also believed the Jews were sub-human*. The earnestness of their belief did not alter the humanity of the Jews; likewise, the adamance of our society's claims does not strip away the humanity from our unborn children. In truth, every abortion performed in this country is the death of a human being.

Socialism and Abortion—Linked?

Planned Parenthood is by far the largest abortion provider in the United States today. How many people know that its founder, Margaret Sanger, began her career as a zealous and outspoken socialist?

Sanger served as a leading member of the Women's Committee for the Socialist Party in New York, and in her early days was active in a revolutionary socialist/anarchist organization called Industrial Workers of the World (IWW). Sanger was a contributing columnist for the socialist magazine *New York Call* and also began her own publication in 1914 called *Woman Rebel*. The tag line for this publication—"No Gods, No Masters"—was a socialist slogan she borrowed from the IWW.

Sanger was, throughout her life, a firm believer in the socialist ideal. This is what fueled her life's work and led to the founding of Planned Parenthood. Sanger believed humanity was capable of attaining a state of civilization characterized by human fulfillment, equality, and harmony—a world free from the shackles of poverty and suffering, where war and oppression would be a dim memory from the past.

Throughout her life Sanger held onto this ideal; although over time (and presumably for self-preservation due to the Red Scare in the United States after the Word Wars), her early Marxist views broadened and "evolved." She, along with many socialists of her time, became disillusioned with orthodox Marxism and concluded that Marx had failed to probe deep enough into the human psyche in his assessment of the causes of human misery. She also felt that Marx's traditional revolutionary remedy—limited to the realm of economics—was too narrow in scope to achieve its desired aims.

In *The Pivot of Civilization* she explains,

> In spite of all my sympathy with the dream of liberated labor, I was driven to ask whether this urging power of sex,

this deep instinct, was not at least partially responsible, along with industrial injustice, for the widespread misery of the world."[45]

She goes on to say,

> In pointing out the limitations and fallacies of the orthodox Marxian opinion, my purpose is not to depreciate the efforts of the Socialists aiming to create a new society, but rather to emphasize what seems to me the greatest and most neglected truth of our day: Unless sexual science is incorporated as an integral part of world-statesmanship and the pivotal importance of Birth Control is recognized in any program of reconstruction, all efforts to create a new world and a new civilization are foredoomed to failure. We can hope for no advance until we attain a new conception of sex, not as a merely propagative act, not merely as a biological necessity for the perpetuation of the race, but as a psychic and spiritual avenue of expression.

> ...No Socialism will ever be possible until the problem of responsible parenthood is solved.[46]

In her estimation, no political and economic liberation could occur until a sexual liberation had been won. The newly formulated contraceptive pill, she believed, was the three-pronged scientific key the world had been waiting for; poised to propel humanity forward toward the socialist ideal.

First, "birth control" (Sanger is the one who coined this phrase) would liberate women forever from the burden of having to mother unwanted and unplanned children. Not only would the resulting fewer mouths to feed eliminate the evils of overcrowding and poverty, but women—finally unshackled from the fetters of motherhood—would be free to pursue their own happiness and self-fulfillment. This would, Sanger believed, benefit society at large and improve quality of life for both men and women...and the children women *wanted* to conceive.

Second, making contraceptive measures more easily and readily available to women of lower classes (predominantly African American at that time) would protect the new civilization from what was, in her "scientific" estimation, its severest and most imminent threat: racial and genetic degeneration. She also called for the forced sterilization to counteract this dire threat.[47]

In a 1912 article she compares human beings of "lower" races than her own with *chimpanzees* and *rapists*:

The lower down in the scale of human development we go the less sexual control we find. It is said that the aboriginal Australian, the lowest known species of the human family, just a step higher than the chimpanzee in brain development, has so little sexual control that police authority alone prevents him from obtaining sexual satisfaction on the streets. According to one writer, the rapist has just enough brain development to raise him above the animal, but like the animal, when in heat knows no law except nature which impels him to procreate whatever the result.[48]

In *The Pivot of Civilization*, she says,

The most urgent problem to-day is how to limit and discourage the over-fertility of the mentally and physically defective. Possibly drastic and Spartan methods may be forced upon American society if it continues complacently to encourage the chance and chaotic breeding that has resulted from our stupid, cruel sentimentalism...

It [Eugenics] sees that the most responsible and the most intelligent members of society are the less fertile; that the feeble-minded are the more fertile. Herein lies the unbalance, the great biological menace to the future of civilization. Are we heading to biological destruction, toward the gradual but certain attack upon the stocks of intelligence and racial health by the sinister forces of the hordes of irresponsibility and imbecility?...

This undervaluation, this cheapening of child life, is to speak crudely but frankly the direct result of overproduction. "Restriction of output" is an immediate necessity if we wish to regain control of the real values, so that unimpeded, unhindered, and without danger of inner corruption, humanity may protect its own health and powers.[49]

This is feminism's greatest hero!

Third and lastly, Sanger believed the pill—which would separate the act of sex from the unwanted effect of sex (children)—would enable humans to more deeply and fully explore the full spiritual potential of their sexuality.

Once we have accomplished the first tentative steps toward the creation of a real civilization, the task of freeing the spirit of mankind from the bondage of ignorance, prejudice, and mental passivity which is fettering more now than ever in the history of humanity, will be facilitated a thousandfold. The great central problem, and the one which must be taken first is the abolition of the shame and fear of sex. ...Through sex, mankind may attain the great spiritual illumination which will transform the world, which will light up the only path to an earthly paradise. So must we necessarily conceive of sex-expression. The instinct is here. None of us can avoid it. It is in our power to make it a thing of beauty and a joy forever: or to deny it, as have the ascetics of the past...[50]

Planned Parenthood was founded to achieve these aims. Sanger and her contemporaries began the fight for a slightly different kind of socialist revolution than that which Marx had envisioned...a revolution that would be marked by peace, love, and "science"...a *Sexual Revolution*.

Yet Another Botched Socialist Revolution

What comes as a shock to those of us living today is the fact that the founder of Planned Parenthood, throughout her career, spoke out *against* abortion. Sanger viewed abortion as barbaric and was (at least publicly) opposed to abortion unless the health of the mother was at risk.

Sanger believed that her efforts to make birth control available to the masses—especially to the poor—would eliminate the need for abortion in this country. She believed that if women could control their own fertility through science, only *planned* offspring would ever be conceived. There would, therefore, be no need to abort pregnancies after conception had occurred. In the new society, abortion would be a disgusting thing of the pre-enlightened past.

She could not have been more wrong.

Her efforts have led in the opposite direction. Her efforts have led directly to a drastic, exponential rise in abortion and also to the legalization of abortion in the United States.

Sanger's new and improved methods of reaching the socialist ideal did not work out as planned.

She succeeded in slowing down population growth, and to this day this hits America's African American population the hardest. (Today more African American babies are aborted in New York City each year than are born alive![51]) Sanger succeeded in separating sex from parenthood in the minds of Americans. She succeeded in separating sex from God's Law and any kind of moral grounding. She succeeded in increasing the number of out-of-wedlock pregnancies in this country. She succeeded in encouraging women to be entitled and selfish.

She did not succeed in eliminating poverty. She did not succeed in freeing the world from oppression. She did not succeed in stopping unwanted pregnancies. She did not succeed in giving women the power to dictate human life.

And she did not succeed in eliminating abortion.

Margaret Sanger's sexual revolution has resulted in the deaths of more human beings than Mao's Cultural Revolution and more deaths of human beings than Hitler's efforts to purge Germany of its uncleanness.

And still, it rages on.

Sanger's attempt to achieve the socialist ideal led straight to death…on a massive scale.

What Comes Next?

Where might death next rise to meet us unaware?

Sanger was convinced that the "science" of birth control and eugenics would solve the world's greatest problems and open up a road to utopia. Could environmentalism be to our generation what the eugenics movement was to socialists of Sanger's generation? Could climate change—the dire, imminent threat currently blocking our civilization from reaching our future destiny—be socialism's next great death trap? How many human lives could over-the-top environmental laws end up sacrificing on the road to "saving" them?

Could COVID-19 quarantine laws and social-distancing, over the long term, turn out to have harmed more human lives than it saved? Could loosening criminal justice laws—all in the spirit of "compassion" and "equality"—put society at large in danger of death by terrorist and criminal activity? Could hate speech laws turn free-thinking people into enemies who have to be destroyed? How far is society willing to take its efforts to stamp systemic racism out of traditional American institutions?

Time will tell, but mark these words: Wherever socialism forges its path, *death is never far behind.*

"My object in life is to dethrone God and destroy capitalism."

—KARL MARX

8

SOCIALISM'S FATAL MISDIAGNOSIS

STRUGGLE & ALIENATION

Sun Tzu believed and taught that the highest art of war is winning the battle subversively; that is, through deception.

He was wrong.

There is a higher art of war he could not see; a higher strategy he failed to comprehend. There is one thing stronger than subversion. One weapon—and only one weapon—that can slice through the power of deception and obliterate it:

Truth.

The only way to escape destruction by socialism is for us to rediscover, re-implement, and fight for the Truth our society has forgotten. To do this effectively, however, we must understand what our society believes.

Class Struggle and Alienation

At the very heart of the socialist movement we see rising in America today are buried two principle concepts that come straight out of the theories of Karl Marx. These two ideas are what he called *class struggle* and *alienation*. Examining these two principles is paramount if we want to understand what is occurring in our culture.

Of course, not all socialists and progressives consider themselves to be Marxists, but the democratic socialist revolution presently rising in our country nevertheless has its roots firmly planted in Marxist theory and ideology.

The Merriam-Webster Learner's Dictionary defines Marxism very simply as "the political, economic, and social theories of Karl Marx including the belief that the *struggle between social classes* is a major force in history and that there should eventually be a society in which there are no classes."[52]

What Karl Marx—the father of modern socialism—encountered, when he opened his eyes to the world around him, was suffering. He saw pain everywhere he looked. He saw inequality, injustice, hunger, poverty, bondage, war, and oppression. He saw *struggle*. He observed that for all of history mankind has been and is forever engaged in a ceaseless, bitter *struggle*.

He also observed something else: *alienation*.

It seemed to him that many people are alienated in their work; that is, they are unable to engage in the sort of labor that is truly fulfilling and meaningful to them. He noticed that people are also *alienated*, or separated and divided, from other human beings.

Bertell Ollman, Professor of Politics at NYU, writes, on alienation, "The distortion in what Marx takes to be human nature is generally referred to in language which suggests that an *essential tie* has been cut in the middle."[53] Marx refers to alienation as "a mistake, a defect, which ought not to be."[54]

Why is life hard? Why is work so unfulfilling? Why do war, oppression, poverty, hunger, and crime exist? Where do all the problems of our world *originate?*

That was the question Marx was trying to answer.

Marx, like many Americans today, was an atheist and materialist who rejected the idea of the existence of immaterial realities such as God and human souls or spirits. He did not believe in what traditional Christianity would call a "sin nature."

The only conclusion he could ultimately draw, then, was that human nature is corrupted by something *outside* of man. Corruption must be a *material* problem.

Bernie Sanders was echoing this same belief, prevalent all across our society today, when he said, "I believe most of the crime we see is a result of people's economic condition."[55]

The *great struggle* of humanity, according to Marx, comes from the financial or material gap that exists between "owner" and the "employee," the "exploiter" and the "exploited," the "rich" and the "poor," the "ruling class" and the "working class," the "bourgeoisie" and the "proletariat," the "1%" and "the rest of us," the "privileged" and the "oppressed"— and the conflicting economic interests of these two groups, however you want to label them. Thus he named the most basic, foundational struggle of humanity "class struggle." (And remember, his definition of "oppression" was based on the now-disproved labor theory of value.)

According to Marx, *alienation*, or dissatisfaction and lack of fulfillment in labor, as well as disunity and separation between people, is also caused by the material chasm that exists between the rich and the poor, and specifically by the division of labor that emerges as capitalist economies thrive and grow.

Now, if the greatest problems of humanity are caused by this *material or financial gap between classes*, then *capitalism*, an economic system which allows some to become wealthy owners of means of production while others remain lesser-paid employees, is responsible for causing humanity's deepest suffering.

Marx also believed that a society's beliefs, values, and institutions all arise and grow out of its *economic reality*. He believed that humans *create* religions, belief systems, and social/political institutions to help them make sense of their economic condition—and that they construct them with the primary aim of protecting the economic interests of the "ruling class" and keeping the "exploited class" held down. [56] Institutions like the police force, the military, and legal system *enforce* capitalist laws and ideas; institutions like religion, family, and education *teach* them.

Thus, in Marxist ideology, a capitalist society's institutions and traditional beliefs are an integral part of the human problem. They *perpetuate* class struggle and alienation. Marx wrote, "But the essence of man is no abstraction inherent in each single individual. In reality, it is the ensemble of the social relations."[57]

Another Point of View

It just so happens that in the very first pages of the Bible we come face to face with these same two foundational human problems Karl Marx observed: *struggle* and *alienation*.

The Bible, however, offers a vastly different explanation for the bitter realities of *struggle* and *alienation* in our world. It points to a very different cause for all the pain, injustice, inequality, hunger, poverty, bondage, war, and oppression we see around us; for the separation and loneliness that exists between people; and for the seemingly inescapable difficulty and futility of our work.

In the beginning, when God first created the world and the world's first two human beings, man himself, man's environment, and all of his relationships were *perfect*.

> So God created human beings in his own image. In the image of God he created them; male and female he created them. Then God blessed them and said, "Be fruitful and multiply. Fill the earth and govern it. Reign over the fish in the sea, the birds in the sky, and all the animals that scurry along the ground. Then God said, "Look! I have given you every seed-

bearing plant throughout the earth and all the fruit trees for your food. And I have given every green plant as food for all the wild animals, the birds in the sky, and the small animals that scurry along the ground—everything that has life." And that is what happened. Then God looked over all he had made, and he saw that it was very good! Genesis 1:27-31a

There was no *struggle* in the beginning. Pain, hunger, and injustice didn't exist! There was no hate, oppression, poverty, or war. The earth was filled with plenty and it was good.

There was also no *alienation*.

The first two human beings existed in perfect harmony...

1. **first and foremost, with God.**
   Adam and Eve had open and complete access to God. They talked with Him and dwelt in His presence; God's face was not hidden! In Genesis 3:8 we read that *God walked in the Garden* with Adam and Eve.

2. **with their own identities as man and woman.**
   "God created man in His own image, in the image of God He created him; male and female He created them." Genesis 1:27

   "...It is not good for the man to be alone; I will make him a helper who is just right for him." Genesis 2:18

   Adam and Eve knew themselves and each other inside and out. They knew their place in the universe; they understood their true identity as limited, created beings existing under the authority of a loving God. God created man and woman as two equally valuable but very different people with unique genders and complementary roles in marriage. In the beginning, this uniqueness wasn't a burden; it didn't feel unfair. There was no power struggle. Gender was designed by God and it was beautiful. It was *good*.

3. with their children.

The very first command God gave Adam and Eve was this: "Be fruitful and multiply. Fill the earth and govern it." Genesis 1:28 Adam and Eve were told that their first and most important job was to bear and raise children! They were supposed to multiply; to train up their children to be God's appointed kings and queens on this earth—reigning over the earth on His behalf and under His authority. What a calling!

4. with each other.

Adam and Eve's naked existence together as human beings with no shame was evidence of this perfect unity. Not even a stitch of clothing separated their pure harmony. "And the man and his wife were both naked and were not ashamed." Genesis 2:25 This unity was birthed first and foremost within marriage and was meant to overflow outward into family, society, and the world.

5. with their work.

Adam's labor was easy, fruitful, and fulfilling. We read,

The Lord God planted a garden toward the east, in Eden; and there He placed the man whom He had formed. Out of the ground the Lord God caused to grow every tree that is pleasing to the sight and good for food; the tree of life also in the midst of the garden, and the tree of the knowledge of good and evil. Then the Lord God took the man and put him into the garden of Eden to cultivate it and keep it. Genesis 2:8, 9, 15

Adam was given a clear job to do, and his work was a joy. There were no thorns, no weeds, no blistering heat to hold him back.

6. with their environment.

God gave Adam and Eve a privileged position. He told Adam and Eve to "fill the earth, and subdue it; and rule over the fish of the sea and over the birds of the sky and over every living thing that moves on the earth." Genesis 1:28b (NASB) They were God's elected rulers over the earth and were to utilize its richness for the good of mankind and the glory of God. There were no destructive storms, no draughts, no floods, and no extreme temperatures to worry about. Wild animals weren't a threat. Everything in the environment worked in perfect symmetry and harmony for the benefit of mankind.

7. and with no fear of death!

Adam and Eve were created to be immortal. They were meant to live forever with all of their descendants in this beautiful Garden. Death did not exist. It was nowhere to be seen! They lived happy, joyful, peaceful lives without any fear of death lurking over their heads.

The world as God created it was a perfect paradise. It was a place of peace, safety, fulfillment, and harmony. God *created institutions!* They are not merely human creations that grow out man's economic condition. God began the world with *law* and *family*, and these institutions were good.

But something terrible happened to mankind, and this earth. Something truly catastrophic occurred that would change the course of history forever:

Sin entered the human heart.

God had given Adam and Eve one simple law: "But the Lord God warned him, "You may freely eat the fruit of every tree in the garden—except the tree of the knowledge of good and evil. If you eat its fruit, you are sure to die." Genesis 2:16, 17

Take a look at what happened next:

The serpent was the shrewdest of all the wild animals the Lord God had made. One day he asked the woman, "Did God really say you must not eat the fruit from any of the trees in the garden?"

"Of course we may eat fruit from the trees in the garden," the woman replied. "It's only the fruit from the tree in the middle of the garden that we are not allowed to eat. God said, 'You must not eat it or even touch it; if you do, you will die.'"

"You won't die!" the serpent replied to the woman. "God knows that your eyes will be opened as soon as you eat it, and you will be like God, knowing both good and evil."

The woman was convinced. She saw that the tree was beautiful and its fruit looked delicious, and she wanted the wisdom it would give her. So she took some of the fruit and ate it. Then she gave some to her husband, who was with her, and he ate it, too. Genesis 3:1-6

Satan—the father of lies—constructs here his first web of deception for humans. He has one object and one object alone: *to seduce mankind to trade the Law of God for slavery and death.*

All Satan had to do was to plant a seed of doubt in Eve's mind. He challenged the Eternal Truth she had heard for herself from God's mouth. Satan tempted Eve to throw off the constriction of God's Law and to follow a different path than the one God had laid out for her. He promised her freedom and power in return!

Eve was not forced to sin. She *chose* to sin.

Satan deceived Eve, and she fell for it. She then passed the Lie on over to Adam, and he fell for it, too. Eve first, and then Adam, each individually made a conscious choice to disobey God's clear command.

Satan had promised them freedom, but what they got instead was slavery, pain, and death. They got *struggle* and *alienation*. Sin darkened their hearts, and human nature was corrupted forever. An essential tie was, indeed, cut in the middle.

This is what happened:

1. The worst effect of sin was that **it alienated mankind from the presence of God.** Tainted by sin as they now were, Adam and Eve could no longer live within the holy and pure presence of God. Mankind would forever bear in their very hearts, their very nature, a black mark of sin that would separate them from God. Our first parents were expelled from Paradise and the way of return was blocked. *There was no going back.*

   > "...therefore the Lord God sent him out from the garden of Eden, to cultivate the ground from which he was taken. So He drove the man out; and at the east of the garden of Eden He stationed the cherubim and the flaming sword which turned every direction to guard the way to the tree of life." Genesis 3:23, 24

2. Because Eve had taken the lead in disobeying God and led her husband to join her in eating the forbidden fruit, **Eve's identity and role as a woman, which was created to be a beautiful gift and source of fulfillment for her, was cursed.** It became a source of contention between her and her husband. "To

the woman [God] said...your desire will be for your husband, and he will rule over you." Genesis 3:16

It was when sin entered the world that conflict and confusion surrounding roles and identity sprang up. Harmony within marriage and between the sexes would be a struggle from that time onward. Man would be tempted to take advantage of his role as leader and woman would struggle with jealousy over her husband's role.

3. Adam and Eve's **job as parents became difficult and painful:** "I will greatly multiply your pain in childbirth, in pain you will bring forth children." Genesis 3:16

It would be a painful struggle to bring children into this world; parents would have to fight and work hard to raise their children up to be the men and women they were created to be.

4. After they sinned, Adam and Eve were immediately overcome by shame. For the first time in their existence, they realized they were naked. **Their perfect intimacy and unity were broken; they had become alienated from each other.** They hurried to hide; to cover their nakedness from one another and from God: "Then the eyes of both of them were opened, and they knew that they were naked; and they sewed fig leaves together and made themselves loin coverings." Genesis 3:7

It would only take one generation for this devastating seed of division among human beings to turn into such a dark hatred that it would lead to the first murder (Genesis 4).

5. **Their labor became tedious and difficult; they were alienated in their work.**

And to the man He said, "Since you listened to your wife and ate from the tree whose fruit I commanded you not to eat, the ground is cursed because of you. All your life you will struggle to scratch a living from it. It will grow thorns and thistles for you, though you will eat of its grains. By the sweat of your brow will you have food to eat..." Genesis 3:17-19a

No longer would mankind's labor be pure joy. It would be difficult and tedious for man to make a living to survive.

6. **The environment became hostile.** Planet Earth changed when sin entered the world. The earth itself became cursed and started to work against mankind. Animals turned vicious. Now there was hunter and prey, death, and decay. Disease and disaster became threats. Sorrow and suffering appeared on the face of the earth.

And most horrible of all,

7. **Death entered the world.** The Bible teaches that the penalty for sin is death. Because of Adam and Eve's sin, an animal had to be killed to cover the shame of human sin: "The Lord God made garments of skin for Adam and his wife, and clothed them." Genesis 3:21. Now, because of their sin, Adam and Eve would face death themselves as well. They would not live forever as God had originally planned: "...till you return to the ground, because from it you were taken; for you are dust, and to dust you shall return." Genesis 3:19b

Marx was absolutely correct when he noted that in man's nature some "essential tie has been cut in the middle;" but his materialistic view of the world led him to a wrong assessment of *what that tie was* and *how it was cut.*

We must not follow his catastrophic mistake! The *essential tie* which was cut was man's harmonious relationship with God… and it was severed by *sin.*

God says that the *great struggle* and the *alienation* we see in our world is *not* at its core a material struggle between the rich and the poor or between any other "classes" or groups in society, as socialism would have us believe.

The human problem is a spiritual problem caused by the dark presence of sin in individual human hearts.

> "For from the heart come evil thoughts, murder, adultery, all sexual immorality, theft, lying, and slander. These are what defile you." Matthew 15:19, 20a

> "How can I know the sins lurking in my heart? Cleanse me from these hidden faults." Psalm 19:12

Socialism lays all the blame for human misconduct and pain on economics and social systems and institutions, but in reality, these problems stem from the struggle with sin that rages inside every individual human heart.

Your heart and mine.

Karl Marx started with a fatal miscalculation regarding the basic problem facing mankind, and from there he only diverged further from God's Truth in his plan for a solution.

"Marxism is a Christian heresy."

—FRANCIS SCHAEFFER

SOCIALISM'S DIABOLICAL SOLUTION

REVOLUTION!

What is Marx's solution to humanity's greatest problems? Revolution! He calls for the complete destruction of the existing social order. He writes,

> Between capitalist and communist society lies the period of the revolutionary transformation of the one into the other. There corresponds to this also a political transition period in which the state can be nothing but the revolutionary dictatorship of the proletariat.[58]

Marx believed it was only a matter of time before civilization would move past capitalism to form a new, classless society. Such a progression was, in his mind, inevitable. Once the oppressed class ("the proletariat") was made conscious of the oppressive nature of capitalism, they would rise, struggle against, and overthrow their oppressors (" the bourgeoisie") to rip away their wealth and power:

> The proletariat will use its political supremacy to wrest, by degree, all capital from the bourgeoisie, to centralise all instruments of production in the hands of the State, *i.e.*, of the proletariat organised as the ruling class; and to increase the total productive forces as rapidly as possible...

If by means of a revolution it makes itself the ruling class and, as such, sweeps away by force the old conditions of production, then it will, along with these conditions, have swept away the conditions for the existence of class antagonisms and of classes generally.[59]

Marx viewed class struggle as *the* means by which economic and social changes in a society are made. If we end capitalism, if we drastically redistribute wealth equally across society, and if we allow the *collective* rather the *individual* to make all economic and social decisions, then the bitter human problems of struggle and alienation will finally end.

Paul D'Amato, a writer for *Socialist Worker*, summarizes this belief concisely: "In other words, in changing their environment, human beings change themselves."[60]

Under socialism, wars will cease. No group of people within society will ever be held down. No one will be tempted by a financial incentive to destroy the planet. There will be no more need to steal or fight. No one will get stuck in a job they don't like.

To achieve this in the United States, all we have to do is *completely destroy every aspect of traditional America.*

As we already discovered, last century's communist revolutions were revolutions of violence. America's democratic socialist revolution has, up until very recently, been a revolution of subversion. But both versions have the same underlying goal: to destroy capitalism and all the institutions, laws, thought patterns, and values that support it.

It just so happens that the values that support capitalism (individual human rights, the existence of a higher law, a work ethic that relies on individual reward and responsibility, investment that leads to profit, and the subjective theory of value) are values that originate in the Bible. The traditional family as God has defined it and the institution of the Christian church stand as two of the greatest natural enemies of socialism because their teachings stand in the way of everything socialists believe. In every socialist revolution, there comes a time when socialists realize that to reach their goal they have no choice but to silence Christians and criminalize the teachings of the Bible.

The False Religion of Socialism

Socialism is, in reality, a counterfeit Christianity. It is a religion all in itself that seeks to *replace* Christianity. Socialism offers an alternative explanation of what evil is and where evil comes from; it also outlines an alternative method for overcoming it. Socialism demands that we sacrifice and destroy everything we own to cleanse our society from corruption. A socialist revolution is a ritual sacrifice.

It requires us to give up our culture, our history, our foundations of law and order, our religious beliefs, our wealth, our liberty, our conception of family, and our identity as human beings. In the end, it even tells us we have to destroy humanity itself.

But the Bible tells us we don't have the power to right all the wrongs in our society. Humans are not capable of improving human nature or creating a perfected civilization. Even if we sacrificed everything we owned it wouldn't be enough, because Paradise comes at a price humanity can't afford. Paradise demands a *perfect* sacrifice, and none of us has a perfect sacrifice to give.

The problems and struggles that exist in our society don't stem from material imbalances between the rich and the poor, and they don't come from capitalism and traditional American institutions. They come from *within us.*

Our own individual hearts are flawed and they are filthy.

God's solution for the problems of struggle and alienation in this world is, as you might surmise, the polar opposite of what socialism proposes. God's solution is two-fold. He provides us with a permanent solution to *defeat evil,* and He provides us with a temporary solution to *restrain evil.*

God's Permanent Solution for Defeating Evil

The only way to get rid of evil in this world is for individual hearts to be washed clean—one by one—by the blood of Jesus Christ.

The wonder of Christianity is that Someone already stepped in from the outside and made the ultimate sacrifice *for us!*

Jesus left His riches and His throne in heaven and became poor. He gave up every privilege He rightfully owns as the Son of God and came down to this wretched earth to fight and win the Revolution in our place. He was tortured and He died on a cruel Roman cross for you and me because He knew we could never win the battle against evil on our own. And He did not stay dead! He *rose* from the dead, conquering the power of death and evil forever.

America, this is good news! It means *the Revolution has already been fought and won!* We are trying to defeat corruption in our own strength. We don't understand that evil was already defeated by the Son of God Himself.

We lost Paradise because of the sin that exists in our hearts, but God offers Paradise back to us as a *free gift.* All we need to do is get down on our knees in humility before the loving God of this universe and accept it by faith.

> For this is how God loved the world: He gave his one and only Son, so that everyone who believes in him will not perish but have eternal life. God sent his Son into the world not to judge the world, but to save the world through him. There is no judgment against anyone who believes in him. But anyone who does not believe in him has already been judged for not believing in God's one and only Son. And the judgment is based on this fact: God's light came into the

world, but people loved the darkness more than the light, for their actions were evil. John 3:16-19

Will you turn to Him and accept His gift of forgiveness today? Will you accept the gift of Paradise restored? There's more to this book, but it can wait. If you have never met Jesus Christ before, He wants you to meet Him now. *Meet your Creator.* He is calling your name.

The Prodigal Son by Rembrandt

When God washes our hearts clean, the Bible says we are completely forgiven of all our sins. Our guilt is lifted and our hearts are freed forever from the weight of sin. We still have battles with sin throughout our time here on earth, but we're not *chained* to those sins anymore. *God provides a way out.*

Little by little God starts restoring to us what we lost in Paradise. We rediscover His original design for our lives and He gives us victory after victory over the *personal sin* that screws up our families and society. These victories over sin in our individual lives is what makes this world a better place.

Jesus is the key to real change.

God's Temporary Solution for Restraining Evil

Unfortunately, not everyone wants to have their hearts cleansed by Jesus Christ. And not all of us who believe in Jesus are willing to surrender to Him and align our lives with His Truth. Thus, evil continues to run rampant in human hearts. It overflows into our homes, onto our streets, and out into the world. It morphs into violence. It hurts people.

What can we do about that evil?

God's *temporary* solution to restrain evil on earth is found in the institution of government. Not just any government, however; it needs to be a government that recognizes the threat of man's sinful nature and limits its power by submitting to a Rule of Law higher than itself. This kind of Rule of Law—one that respects God's Eternal Law—is what protects citizens from unrestrained evil.

There is no perfect government or form of government in this fallen world, but the idea of government and justice based on individual responsibility to a higher law was designed by God to establish order within a society. It was designed to protect citizens from violence and tyranny. When a society chooses to accept God's definition of justice, some measure of order and safety can be maintained.

Humanity does, however, have a free choice. We *are* free to let our limited government grow into a monster. We *are* free to snub our noses at the idea of a Higher Law. We *are* free to sit back and watch silently as people rip our God-honoring, humanity-protecting, tyranny-defying government checks and balances and Constitution to shreds.

We need to understand, though, that in doing so we are rejecting the protection plan God offers human beings against tyranny, chaos, and violence; and every one of us will reap the consequences of that choice.

Socialism, Death, and Destruction

The magnitude of evil we find lurking at the core of socialism—after we sift down through all of its layers and strip off its masks—is almost inconceivable.

Through his systematic study of the history of socialism in *The Socialist Phenomenon*, Igor Shafarevich demonstrates that *the impulse of self-destruction plays a real role in human history.* This impulse, he discovers, is a "fundamental and organic part of socialist ideology."[61]

He concludes with this statement: **"The death of mankind is not only a conceivable result of the triumph of socialism—it constitutes the goal of socialism."**[62]

Beneath its smooth and enticing exterior, socialism is pure, raw evil. Aleksandr Solzhenitsyn depicted the spirit of revolution—which ravaged his homeland of Russia—as a great, tall red wheel made of iron, like that attached to a train engine.[63] This wheel caused the total death and destruction of everything in its path.

Solzhenitsyn predicted the red wheel would not be content to stop where it may, at first glance, seem to have halted in the 20th century. He believed it would roll on in an attempt to crush the whole world[64]—and especially Western civilization.[65]

On July 9, 1975, in a speech to the American Federation of Labor and Congress of Industrial Organizations, he warned,

Couldn't it be possible to, ahead of time, to assess soberly the world-wide menace that threatens to swallow the whole world? I was swallowed myself. I have been in the dragon's belly, in its red-hot innards. It was unable to digest me and threw me up. I have come to you as a witness to what it is like there, in the dragon's belly.

...A concentration of world evil is taking place, full of hatred for humanity. It is fully determined to destroy your society.[66]

Could it be that Solzhenitsyn was correct? That last century's wave of communist revolution was only the beginning? I believe last century's experiments with socialism were paving the way for a larger, global brand of socialism that will carry the world right up to the end of time when it is destined to be judged by its Maker. The future may prove me right or wrong, but I know one thing for sure:

Today we, the people of the United States of America, face a choice; it is the choice of *freedom* or *slavery*, the choice of *life* or *death*.

It is the same choice Russia encountered a little over a hundred years ago when socialism came knocking on her door promising social justice and equality. It is the same choice the Chinese faced when Mao promised an escape from poverty and oppression. And it is the same choice the Germans faced when Hitler promised them a perfected civilization.

Indeed, the choice we face today is the same one Adam and Even faced long ago in the Garden of Eden. Socialism dangles all sorts of enticing fruit before our eyes:

- *Protection from sickness, death, and COVID-19.*

- *Salvation from human-induced climate change.*

- *An end to all oppression.*

- *Free money for the poor.*

- *An end to hunger and poverty.*

- *Equality for all through the redistribution of wealth.*

- *Human fulfillment.*

- *Freedom from our outdated Constitution.*

- *Liberty from the restrictions of God's Laws.*

But who are socialists to make such claims when God has commanded once and for all time,

"Thou shalt not covet."

"Thou shalt not steal."

"Thou shalt have no other gods before me."

Which are we, as a nation, going to choose?

The empty promises of man—and slavery? Or the Law of God—and liberty?

"They said, 'Come, let us build for ourselves a city, and a tower whose top will reach into heaven...'"

—GENESIS 11:4A (NASB)

10

SOCIALISM'S FUNDAMENTAL FLAW

WHY HUMANITY CAN'T GET IT RIGHT

Socialists long for a better future. As humanity attains new heights in science, technology, and social awareness, life here on earth, they believe, is destined to improve. There's a new civilization just around the corner. It lies at our very fingertips if only we are enlightened enough to reach out and grasp it! This belief is what fuels revolutionary zeal.

Socialism and the concept of utopia are inseparable. If there is no achievable bright future for tomorrow, there is no socialism. The *extent* of the promises of utopia, however, has fluctuated over time and still varies from one group of socialists to another.

Karl Marx believed utopia would denote the complete end of mankind's struggle and alienation. It would constitute the healing of man's splintered nature, the welding together of that "essential tie" which had been cut. NYU Professor Bertell Ollman writes,

> If alienation is the splintering of human nature into a number of misbegotten parts, we would expect communism [that is, Marx's "true communism" aka "utopia"] to be presented as a kind of reunification. And this is just what we find. On one occasion, Marx asserts that communism is "the

complete return of man to himself as a social (i.e. human) being—a return become conscious, and accomplished with the entire wealth of a previous development." It is "the positive transcendence of all estrangement—that is to say, the return of man from religion, family, state, etc. to his human, i.e. social mode of existence." In communism the breach is healed and all the elements which constitute a human being for Marx are reunited.[67]

Modern socialists present somewhat modified visions of utopia. Ollman gives his own vision:

> Imagine walking down a clean street, encountering friendly people, and knowing that everyone you see has enough to eat and a decent place to live. You do not fear being robbed or otherwise abused, and the only police you see are directing traffic. Imagine that you are going to a job you enjoy, where you are respected, not overworked, and where all your suggestions are taken seriously; and that afterwards you meet with friends to pursue common interests with no worry about educational or medical bills that spoil most of our good times. Is this heaven? No, it's socialism.[68]

Democratic socialists Joseph Schwartz and Jason Schulman write,

> Democratic socialism only promises the possibility of human fulfillment. It cannot guarantee happiness. Human failure will exist under democratic socialism, but suffering will not be imposed by *institutions* over which we have no control.[69]

The Democratic Socialists of America website expounds further:

> Finally, racial/ethnic and sex/gender-based oppressions may well continue in a socialist society. Hence a wide range of programs to dismantle the privileges associated with whiteness, maleness and heteronormativity would have to be

136

developed, and antidiscrimination policies in the workplace and in social organizations would have to be intensified… Democratic socialism, that is, will not be the utopia that many socialists of old imagined. Yet the achievement of a democratic socialist society would nevertheless mark one of the greatest advances in human history. Instead of war, there would be peace; instead of competition, cooperation; instead of exploitation, equality; instead of pollution, sustainability; and instead of domination, freedom.[70]

At most, socialism promises a complete end to struggle and alienation and a return to man's original untainted nature. At the very least, it guarantees human fulfillment and world peace. These are some bold promises! What socialism preaches to its followers is that unified humanity can reach its own version of heaven…*without the help of God.*

Socialism Ignores the Inherent Limitations of Humanity

I believe most socialists have good intentions. They just want to make the world a better place. They just want to spread peace. They just want us all to pull together to try and create something good.

But socialism always leads to the polar opposite of what socialists desire. Why?

Part of the answer is this: Economists have proven beyond a shadow of a doubt that the economics of socialism does not work. Volumes have been written on this subject. In *The Problem with Socialism*, DiLorenzo outlines three of the reasons why socialism is economically impossible:

There is first the *incentive problem* socialism creates (because socialism destroys work ethic).

Then there is the *knowledge problem* inherent in any level of central planning (because no bureaucracy given the power to make economic decisions for the masses can come anywhere close to matching the vast knowledge base of millions of specialized individuals and businesses making their own private economic decisions).

And there is also the *calculation problem* that emerges when artificially-set market prices replace reality-based, free-market prices. (Since free-market prices act as a guiding compass for economic decision-makers such as investors and lenders, removing this compass forces decision-makers to act blindly, leading straight to disaster.) [71]

Buried beneath the economics of socialism, however, lies an another even more basic reason why socialism has repeatedly and horrifically backfired in the past, and why there is no hope of it ever succeeding in the future:
Socialism defies God.

In Genesis chapter 11 God presents us with a fascinating historical account.

Many, many years ago, this chapter tells us, there was a group of people on earth who came up with a noble, high-reaching plan.

Their big idea was this: Let's combine all our labor powers and work collectively for one united dream! If we work together, we can build a civilization like no other. We can build a city where we can all live *together* in peace and unity ("otherwise we will be scattered over the face of the whole earth").

The great city these men of old planned was not to be constructed out of the unique and beautiful stones of the earth God had created. No. *Their* city would be built entirely of the bricks they would create for themselves.

From the heart of their great city would rise a jaw-dropping, awe-inspiring tower—also made of man-made bricks—and this tower would be a tower like none other in history. It would be the grandest structure the world had ever known.

Our tower will reach into heaven, they said. *Through the building of this tower, we will make a name for ourselves. The tower will showcase our own might and power and strength!*

And so, they began digging up mud and molding bricks. Brick after brick after brick they formed and then baked. Each brick was equal; each one looked exactly the same as the one that came before it.

The people slaved and they slaved...together...creating endless identical bricks and piling them one on top of the next. Higher, higher: bricks, bricks, and more bricks! They believed with all their hearts that their unified strength would elevate them to the heavens.

But it never did; because God's Eternal Truth says, "Unless the Lord builds a house, the work of the builders is wasted." Psalm 127:1

God was angry, and He was sad. He could see the evil in their hearts growing taller by the day, right alongside the tower. The entire project was a rebellion against Him. It was willful disobedience against His plan for humanity. (Hadn't God commanded first Adam and then Noah to spread out and "fill the earth"—Genesis 1:28, 9:1?)

God could have annihilated them all then and there, but He didn't. He judged them; but in not destroying them, His judgment was also a great act of mercy. He mercifully intervened and rescued the workers from their pride. He saved them from the pointless effort and also, I believe, from the looming disaster ahead—the disaster of death. Surely as the evil in their hearts grew it would have eventually led to death, for isn't that the true end of all evil schemes?

God, in His great love and mercy, saved mankind from himself by giving him back the stunning gift of *individuality*.

God reminded the brick-building slaves who they really were *and who He really is* by bringing their futile efforts to a sudden halt. God gave each man a new language to speak. He gave each one his own unique culture and a brand new identity. God graciously set the workers free, and humanity lived to see another day.

Satan, furious, has been trying to get humans to finish that tower ever since. *He is still working on that project today.*

Socialism's Fundamental Flaw: Pride

Socialism scoffs at the idea of a Sovereign, Creator God who holds any sort of authority over mankind. It persists in elevating itself above the God of Heaven and mocks Him to His face. Socialism is the outworking of a society's core belief that true liberty is freedom *from* God...rather than freedom *in* and *through* God.

Underneath all the grand promises of socialism, we find... lies.

Lies, lies, and more lies.

Wishful thinking.

Blind hope.

The ignorant pride of foolish human beings who think they are greater than God.

Socialism is the rallying together of humanity to try and exert its own power to fix the problems of this world rather than accepting its inherent limitations and asking for the help of Someone greater than itself.

Fellow citizens of this world, how many more times must we fail in our efforts to save the world before we learn *that we are not strong enough?*

Christianity, we must understand, is not theory. It is not hyperbole. It is practical, tangible, living, unchangeable Truth. Jesus Christ is called the Word of Life. This means that He is the source of all life. *He is life itself* (I John 1:1, 2). When an individual or a nation submits to God's authority and follows His Way, what he discovers is life. We find in Jesus Christ rich, sweet *life*; life that overflows in fullness, freedom, and glory. Peace! Fulfillment! Joy! Love! Healing from our brokenness! Liberty!

But any time we humans, in our pride, turn our backs on God—when we rebel against His Law and His Design—what we are doing is turning our backs on *Life itself*. The only thing united humanity is capable of reaching on its own, apart from God, is *death*.

This is why there is no hope of socialism producing anything except death and destruction. There is no hope of life, liberty, or justice apart from God. "The thief comes only to steal and kill and destroy; I have come that they may have life, and have it to the full." John 10:10 (NIV)

Man cannot fix spiritual problems with material solutions. Socialism is a twisted, dangerous copy of God's Truth. Its utopian dream is a false copy of the true dream for the future *God* has planned for us.

True Utopia

In the first book of the Bible, we read an account of humanity's age-old dream to build an enduring city of peace and a tower that would reach heaven, and we see that man wasn't able to achieve it. The Tower of Babel could arguably be the first account of socialism we have in history. It stands as a warning for the ages.

In the last book of the Bible, we read about *another* dream for an enduring city; only this time it's God's dream, not man's.

We humans can't reach heaven on our own, but it turns out God has been planning all along to *bring heaven down to us!* God's enduring city will not be built of brick but of brilliant stones.

> "...So he took me in the Spirit to a great, high mountain, and he showed me the holy city, Jerusalem, descending out of heaven from God. It shone with the glory of God and sparkled like a precious stone—like jasper as clear as crystal." Revelation 21:10, 11

The Bible promises us that a perfect civilization is coming in the future. A brand new Kingdom! God promises enduring world peace, human fulfillment, and eternal bliss—a complete end to all pain, struggle, and alienation. God's promise for the future is brighter than anything we humans could conceive in our wildest dreams.

The Bible is clear when it comes to the fate of humanity and the future destiny of the earth. It is all outlined for us in Revelation 16-22. In these chapters we learn that Jesus Christ, the Son of God and rightful King of the universe, is returning to earth—this very earth that we know and love—one day soon. The Bible says that when He comes, He will establish a new government and will rule over all the nations of the world.

Right before He returns, however, there will be a set seven-year period of the worst tribulation and suffering the earth has ever known. This will be God's judgment upon the earth and on the people on earth who refused to believe in *His* dream.

At the end of those seven awful years, God will bind Satan and end his reign of deception and terror. Christ Himself will establish a new government on this earth. The Bible says Jesus will reign here as King for 1,000 years, and that there will be peace and perfect justice throughout His reign. *Finally, world peace!*

In the last days, the mountain of the Lord's house will be the highest of all—the most important place on earth. It will be raised above the other hills, and people from all over the world will stream there to worship...The Lord will mediate between peoples and will settle disputes between strong nations far away. They will hammer their swords into plowshares and their spears into pruning hooks. Nation will no longer fight against nation, nor train for war anymore. Micah 4:1, 3

After the 1,000 years are over, God will pour out the remainder of His cup of fury on Satan, on all of Satan's followers, and upon the entire earth. *Not every human being will enter God's glorious Kingdom.* The Bible teaches that all people who refused to accept God's free offer of salvation and forgiveness for their sin will be cast away from God's presence into the Lake of Fire...a literal *Hell*...forever.

Then this earth, which has been so marred and destroyed by the presence of sin, will pass away. God says He will raise up for His children a brand new heaven and a brand new earth—each immeasurably more beautiful and glorious than the first.

Then I saw a new heaven and a new earth, for the old heaven and the old earth had disappeared...

And I heard a loud voice from the throne saying, "Look! God's dwelling place is now among the people, and He will dwell with them. They will be His people, and God Himself will be with them and be their God. He will wipe away every tear from their eyes. There will be no more death or mourning or crying or pain, for the old order of things has passed away." Revelation 21:1a, 3-4

How do we reach this Kingdom? All we have to do is recognize that Jesus' death on the cross is the only sacrifice powerful enough to pay for our sin and then accept His Kingdom as a free gift.

The promise God's Kingdom of peace is not built on thin air, nor the wishful thinking of fallen humanity. It stands unfaltering on the Word and of God and the authority of King Jesus Himself. Do not be deceived. He alone owns the strength and power it takes *to make all things new.*

PART TWO

A CALL TO ACTION: RECLAIM ORDINARY LIVING!

"The simple step of a simple, courageous man is not to take part in the lie. Not to support deceit. Let the lie come into the world—even dominate the world—but not through me."

—ALEKSANDR I. SOLZHENITSYN

11

OPERATION ORDINARY
THE POWER OF TRUTHFUL LIVING

In previous chapters I have many times quoted Aleksandr Solzhenitsyn, Igor Shafarevich, and Yuri Bezmenov—three remarkable Russian men who survived Soviet Communism and emerged with a fire burning in their souls to warn the rest of us about what they had experienced. I was fascinated to discover that by the end of their talks and writings, all three men independently arrived at the same conclusion. They each recommended the same course of action for anyone wanting to take a stand against socialism.

There is only one way to overcome socialism, they said: *You must go back to God.*

"Men have forgotten God," Solzhenitsyn famously declared. "That's why all this has happened."[72]

Shafarevich writes,

The term "atheism" is inappropriate for the description of people in the grip of socialist doctrines. It would be more correct to speak here not of "atheists" but of "God-haters," not of "atheism" but of "theophobia." Such, certainly, is the passionately hostile attitude of socialism toward religion. Thus, while socialism is certainly connected with the loss of religious feeling, it can hardly be reduced to it. The place formerly occupied by religion does not remain vacant; a new lodger appeared. This is the only true source of the active principle of socialism, and the aspect which determines the historical role of this phenomenon.[73]

Bezmenov chimes in:

> The most difficult and at the same time the simplest answer to subversion is to start here [in the demoralization phase] and even before by *bringing back the society to religion.*

> ...All the sophisticated technology and computers will not prevent society from disintegrating and eventually dying out. Have you ever met a person who would sacrifice his life, freedom, for the truth like [material knowledge, i.e. 2x2=4]?

> But millions sacrifice their life, freedom, comfort... everything...for things like *God.* Like *Jesus Christ.* It's an honor! Some martyrs in the Soviet concentration camps died; and they died in peace, unlike those who shouted, "Long live Stalin!"

> Something which is *not material* moves society and helps it to survive. So the answer to ideological subversion, strangely enough, is very simple. You don't have to shoot people, you don't have to aim missiles....You simply have to have faith! Strike with the power of your spirit and moral superiority. If you don't have that power, it's high time to develop it. And that's the only answer. That's it.[74]

Throughout the Old Testament, we read account after account of nations that rebelled against God. Ancient Israel rebelled against God. All the pagan nations rebelled against God. Rebellion and hatred for God is humanity's broken and pathetic story, repeated again and again.

In the Old Testament, before raining down judgment on the wicked, God sent prophets to warn the nations. Over and over God said, *Destruction is coming! No one can get away with mocking My Name forever. You are about to feel the full weight of My fury! Your nation is about to collapse!*

But God's warning was always coupled with an invitation. *If you humble yourselves; if you turn away from your sin and pride and turn back to Me, I will forgive you. Repent! I will show great mercy. I will turn away My fierce anger. I will heal your land.* "If I announce that a certain nation or kingdom is to be uprooted, torn down, and destroyed, but then that nation renounces its evil ways, I will not destroy it as I had planned." Jeremiah 18:7, 8

More often than not, God's prophets were mocked and ignored. Most nations ignored all the warnings God sent and continued marching straight into the catastrophic results of their sin.

But sometimes…sometimes…*the people actually listened.*

The citizens of Ninevah, for example, took notice when the prophet Jonah landed on their beach with seaweed in his hair. Immediately upon hearing God's words spoken through Jonah, the wicked Ninevites turned their hearts to God and started living His way instead of their way.

As a result, their city was saved.

God hasn't changed since the days of the Old Testament. His words of warning—and promise—are the same today as they were then. He has warned us in years past. He is warning us now. And He is inviting us to run to the safety of His arms.

How we respond to Jesus Christ today affects not only our eternal future in heaven or hell. It affects our physical lives on this earth and our children's lives, as well. It affects the trajectory of this nation. It affects the future history of the world.

What will we do with Jesus today?

This is the first question we must answer. Will we be like the nations in history who refused to listen and marched themselves straight into God's judgment? Or will we be like the few who actually listened to God's words and *turned around?*

As personal sin and rebellion in this country rise, the lie of socialism swells and grows with it. Its deception is ravaging our society, infiltrating our churches and schools, and taking over our government.

We must act now.

For the past several years, as my husband and I have come to terms with the realities we see unfolding in this country, we have prayed the same prayer repeatedly: *God, we believe. We believe! What do You want us to do?*

Morning after morning, since returning from China four years ago, I have been on my knees in my closet with my Bible open in front of me, pleading with God and searching for wisdom and guidance for these darkening days.

The answer I have found in His Word has been two-fold:

1. Live the Truth

   Live an ordinary life—an ordinary life of Truth—with all your might. Live ordinary. Fiercely, resolutely ordinary.

   Amos 5:21-24; I Peter 1:13-15; John 16:13; Psalm 119:160; Esther 3:2; Daniel 3:17, 18; Daniel 6:10; Exodus 24:7; Deuteronomy 4:6; Nehemiah 3:28-30; Jeremiah 29:4-7; Micah 6:8.

2. Resist Evil

   This is not peacetime, this is war; and Truth is a sword—use it! You must act on the Truth and fight against evil. Refusal to stand up and take action on the Truth is to sit in agreement with the Lie.

   Ezekiel 3:18-21; 2 Corinthians 10:3-5; Isaiah 54:17; Ephesians 6:10-19; 2 Timothy 2:3, 9, 4:2; Psalm 44:5; I Samuel 17:48, 49; Esther 4:12-14; Romans 12:21; James 4:7; Revelation 1:9.

Now, my fellow Americans, I want to pass on God's challenge to you.

1. Live the Truth

Live the Truth? *Live ordinary?* At first, my husband and I struggled to understand exactly what this meant. Like Naaman in the Bible, who chafed at Elisha's simple and humble prescription for healing, we resisted this answer. In the face of such overwhelming and quickly spreading darkness we were expecting God to ask us to do something a little bigger, a little more radical—something more *extraordinary.*

But as we began to obey, and dove into a very ordinary life in a very ordinary house in a very ordinary town, a slow understanding of the significance of what God was calling us to do began to awaken within us.

You see, what socialism is ripping out from the heart of our society is all of our beautiful *ordinary.*

It steals our everyday color, warmth, and strength. Our faith, first of all; our principles and our values, our sweet freedom, and our family life. It seeks to destroy our culture, our patriotism, our history, our abundance, our language, our laughter, and our art.

"In God We Trust" was once the bedrock of our society, but today *ordinary* Christian culture is quickly disappearing from America. Only as it teeters at the brink of destruction do we begin to grasp in full just how precious and extraordinary our *ordinary* really is.

We have to preserve it; and the only way to preserve it is by *living it* with all our might; and in so doing, passing it down to our children and grandchildren.

When I say *living ordinary*, I don't mean merely continuing on the path we've already been traveling; quite the opposite.

I do not mean "business as usual."

Ordinary living means two things. It means *humbling ourselves before God* and it means *realigning our lives with His Eternal Truth.*

Humbling Ourselves Before God

Ordinary living is, first of all, *not extraordinary*.

Not exceptional.

Small. Simple. *Not great.*

We Americans all have a savior complex. We are ready to change the world!

The Left is going to save the world from climate change and inequality. The Right is going to make America great again. Christians are going to go out and do big things for God.

Ordinary living means getting down on our knees and begging God to help us understand one very important fact:

Only God is great.

We humans are not great.

Only God is great.

We are limited. We are finite. We are powerless.

We are small.

Only God is great.

Has the Lord ever needed anyone's advice? Does he need instruction about what is good? Did someone teach Him what is right or show him the path of justice?

Haven't you heard? Don't you understand? Are you deaf to the words of God—the words he gave before the world began? Are you so ignorant? God sits above the circle of the earth. The people below seem like grasshoppers to him!...

He judges the great people of the world and brings them all to nothing. They hardly get started, barely taking root, when he blows on them and they wither. The wind carries them off like chaff. (from Isaiah 40)

Only God is great.

God does great things—amazing things, miraculous things. He does them every single day. He can accomplish great things in and through this nation once again. He can even do great things through ordinary Americans like you and me.

But apart from Him, we can do nothing.

If we are unwilling to get down on our knees before God and humble ourselves today, God will be forced to humble us the hard way. All our military power, all our economic reforms, and all our elections are meaningless if we do not recognize the greatness of God and the smallness of man. "The sacrifices of God are a broken spirit; A broken and a contrite heart, O God, You will not despise." Psalm 51:17 (NASB)

Ordinary living means laying down the illusion of our greatness and offering Him only our smallness, our weakness, and our neediness.

Aligning Our Lives With God's Eternal Truth

Ordinary living also includes something else. After we have humbled ourselves, it means rediscovering and actively putting into practice what *God says is ordinary*—as revealed to us in His Word, the Bible.

It means, in biblical terms, *repenting*. It means turning away from sin and lies and realigning our lives with the Truth of God's Word.

Ordinary living is *truthful living.*

As Bezmenov so clearly demonstrated,[75] socialist ideological subversion has been actively at work pumping lies into our culture for decades. It has attacked and dismantled our families and our society patiently and persistently, one stone at a time.

If we—any of us, no matter how strong or spiritual we think we are—go on assuming we have come through this long struggle unscathed and untouched by the Lie, we are tragically naïve.

When we are deceived, we don't know we are deceived.

I have loved God since I was a little girl, yet I keep discovering areas in my own life and thinking where the lies so prevalent in our world have twisted my perception of reality.

Today we all must open ourselves up to the possibility that maybe, just maybe, we have been wrong. We have to be willing to admit where we have gone wrong, and turn back to God's Truth.

2. Resist Evil

Living the Truth is critical, but our mission doesn't end there. We also have to *raise the Truth like a sword and march into battle with it.*

Some of us Christians have convinced ourselves that fighting against socialism isn't our job; that it is *wrong* for Christians to get tangled up in what is perceived as a purely political debate. We believe it is unloving, unwise, and shameful for us to get inside that boat and start rocking it. After all, *we might offend someone who needs the "love" of Jesus.*

I hope by now we all realize that fighting socialism is not foremost a political battle at all. It is to its very core a spiritual battle. Socialism is an all-out war against God. It is an all-out war against Truth. It is an all-out war against God's people. It is an all-out war against humanity.

What has happened to our moral resolve to be willing to suffer for what is right? Where is our faith that God will take care of us? In my own experience, I have heard only one pastor speak openly and publicly against the lies of socialism and cultural Marxism. *One!*

Dear friends, we cannot afford to remain silent. The good news is that when we stand with God, *to fight is to win.* It is only in our failure to raise our swords that we can ever lose. *We must fight.*

God's eyes are sweeping this nation, searching for Americans who are willing to choose *His ordinary* over our society's "ordinary," and live it, day after ordinary day, with all their might. In peacetime, in war…in isolation, in community…

in acceptance, in rejection...in safety, in persecution...on the mountain, in the valley...always and forever the same, beautiful *ordinary* He has outlined for us in His Word.

I believe God is also searching for ordinary Americans willing to actively oppose the lies of this age, using whatever gifts, talents, resources, and opportunities God gives them.

In Germany, in the fall of 1932 just months before Hitler was appointed Chancellor, pastor and theologian Dietrich Bonhoeffer (who would years later be killed by the Nazis for aiding in a plot to assassinate Hitler) gave a series of lectures at Berlin University.

While most German Christians and churches were caving in to social and political pressures to make compromises in their beliefs, Bonhoeffer was calling them out on it. He stood firm.

A student later recalled some of his words:

> He pointed out that nowadays we often ask ourselves whether we still need the Church, whether we still need God. But this question, he said, is wrong. We are the ones who are questioned. The Church exists and God exists, and we are asked whether we are willing to be of service, for God needs us.[76]

What would have happened in Germany if in 1932 more Germans had said "yes" to God's call?

God must have wept that there were so few! "I looked for someone who might rebuild the wall of righteousness that guards the land. I searched for someone to stand in the gap in the wall so I wouldn't have to destroy the land, but I found no one." Ezekiel 22:30

What would have happened if the few like Bonhoeffer who *did* say yes, leaving us such an astounding example of courage, faith, and nobility, *hadn't?*

Bonhoeffer's rebuke rings true for us today. God is questioning us. *Are we willing?* Because there is only one way we can push back against the darkness rising in our world today. There is only one way to overcome it:

By believing, living, and proclaiming the unchanging Truth of the Living God, regardless of the cost.

And friends, we may as well be honest with ourselves. There will be a cost. As one fellow prisoner used to cheerfully repeat to Solzhenitsyn as they suffered together in the Gulag, "To *stand up* for the truth is nothing! For truth, you must *sit* in jail!"[77]

∾o∾

The lie of socialism contradicts every major aspect of the beautiful, *ordinary* design God laid out for human beings in the first pages of Genesis. Democratic socialism specifically rails against what God says about **our identity as man and woman, our role as parents, our relationship with our neighbors, our true mission as the Church, our attitude toward our work, and our calling when it comes to the environment.**

In the next six chapters, we'll explore how *reclaiming God's ordinary* in each of these areas of our lives can help reverse the effects democratic socialist subversion has had on American life and culture.

"Through the call of Jesus men become individuals...Every man is called separately, and must follow alone. But men are frightened of solitude, and they try to protect themselves from it by merging themselves in the society of their fellow-men and in their material environment...But all this is only a cloak to protect them from having to make a decision. They are unwilling to stand alone before Jesus and to be compelled to decide with their eyes fixed on Him alone."

—DIETRICH BONHOEFFER

12

ORDINARY LIVING...

AS MAN AND WOMAN

"So God created human beings in His own image. In the image of God He created them; male and female He created them."

Genesis 1:27

The first step in living ordinary according to God's Truth is putting our trust in Jesus Christ to forgive our sin and to restore our lost relationship with God. Ordinary living cannot happen if we reject Jesus. We humans can't discover God's ordinary until our sinful hearts have been cleansed and made new through Jesus Christ. So the first step is believing that Jesus is who He says He is.

The next step is discovering who God says *we* are.

Socialism seeks to destroy human identity. As we have learned, the four strands of the red thread of socialism (the abolition of private property, the abolition of the family, the abolition of religion, and communality/equality) attack and undermine *individuality*.

The deeper we wade into socialism, the more we lose all conception of who we truly are as human beings. Our culture currently has an obsession with self-discovery, self-experiment, and self-expression. We are desperate to figure out who we really are and will leave no stone unturned in our quest to get to know ourselves...except, tragically, *the one Stone that has all the answers!*

The path to understanding our true selves must start and end with God. The more we get to know God and dig into His Word, the more we get to know ourselves. In Genesis 1:27 God helps us get started with three monumental facts we need to know about our identity as human beings. This verse tells us that we are *created* beings; that we are created *in the image of God;* and that each one of us is created either *male or female.*

Created

The very first thing God wants you and me to understand about ourselves is that we are *created* beings.

Ordinary living all flows from this one astounding Truth that we did not arrive on this earth by chance; but were designed and formed carefully and artfully by a brilliant, wise, and loving Creator. This changes everything! We are not just blobs of nothing. We are valuable! We are *art!* We are known and loved by Someone greater than ourselves.

If we cannot accept the Truth that God created us, we will never discover any of the beautiful ordinary God designed for us. If we reject the Bible's account of Creation there's no point in going one step further. We have caved in to the Lie already.

God's ordinary starts with Creation.

Created In the Image of God

Not only are human beings created by God; they are also created *in the image of God.* This fact, too, has life-changing ramifications for how we go about our ordinary lives. God created plants and animals, stars, and seas...but none of those things had the privilege, the honor, the special joy of being created *in the image of God.* Mankind is different from the rest of creation. We are set apart. We are unique.

Physically, spiritually, and emotionally, we resemble God. We have special abilities to reason, to create, to love...because God has made us according to His own image. This gives us tremendous, untouchable value. Our worth as human beings is not dependent on race, gender, economic status, health, age, productivity, or any other variable. You want to fight racism and take a stand for justice? Teach Genesis! Every single person on this earth is valuable and important to God. Every human being is worthy of dignity and respect. Every human being is special.

Created Male and Female

So God created the earth and skies: the sun, moon, and stars, and then He created the waters and filled land and sea to the brim with all variety of beautiful plants and creatures. The final being He created was man. He created the first man who ever existed and named him Adam.

Man was the grand finale!

...Almost!

God saw that His work wasn't yet complete.

It wasn't good for Adam to be alone. So God also created Eve.

The two of them together, man and wife, became the crowning glory of God's creation. They were given a great command, a high calling that rings out throughout all ages: *Fill the earth with children!* Multiply! Raise within your home a God-loving family that will multiply into more God-loving families.

Man and woman, each one holding distinct value and created separately in the image of God, were joined together and crowned with the gift of children to become the complete reflection of God's fullness and beauty: family.

Family is God's great masterpiece.

And family, God's way, begins with one individual man and

one individual woman.

In all this world, there is nothing that should be more *ordinary*…so natural and easy to understand…than gender. At the moment of birth, the first and most foundational fact we learn about any child's identity—from their very anatomy—is whether he or she is a boy or a girl.

How the world has managed to make this complicated, I have no idea. But it has, and I know this is painfully difficult for many people.

The truth is, who we are is a gift to the world.

Our gender is a gift from God!

In our quest for *ordinary living* according to God's design, we have to begin at the very beginning. We have to realign our families with this revolutionary idea that men are men and women are women.

What a relief that *we don't have to figure this out on our own!* Our true selves always come to light when we surrender to God's design.

This true identity of ours…the wonders of our God-given gender as well as our unique personality and giftedness as image-bearers of God…are in general designed to be expressed and showcased to their full advantage within marriage.

One man and one woman—so extraordinarily different, but so perfectly complimentary—joined and working together in sacrificial love and harmony? Nothing in this world is more powerful—or more dearly-won—than a godly marriage reflecting God's design.

It's time to start living ordinary again.

If you don't even know where to start; if you don't know what it means to be a man or to be a woman—if you have never had an example or anyone to teach you—find someone who has and ask for help. *That's what community is for.*

Men, it is right for you to reclaim your own identity as a man. It is good. *It is necessary.* You don't have to relinquish your manhood. You don't have to hand it over. *Live it!*

Women of America, we are tired, fragmented, and sad. It's because we have swallowed the Lie. God wants us to find true rest, peace, and fulfillment; but to get there we have to embrace who we are as women. We were not created to fulfill all the roles of a functioning family. We are life-givers. We are caregivers. We are nurturers. We are stunning creators of warmth and beauty! We are many other things, too; but our uniqueness as women needs to be celebrated, embraced, and lived out to its fullest potential—not repressed, starved, and muted.

Marriage Roles: the Road to Stability

Roles. I can sense all the bristles raising, and believe me, I understand, because I have had to go to war against the same defenses in my own heart. I have had to allow God to subdue the resistance in me first before I could ever begin to write this page. And I will tell you some days the bristles still go up and I have to lay them down all over again.

But roles within marriage are critical for us to examine because they are the bedrock and foundation of all of the rest of society. If we ourselves are unwilling to submit to God's design right here, within the realm of our personal identity and inside our own marriages, why do we presume that we will ever see God's design reflected in any other part of our society?

Societal change starts here.

The ordinary, natural Truth of human existence states that God has designed each family member to uniquely fill a special role; *a role only they can fill.* This creates order in families, which benefits and stabilizes not only that family, but all of society. The Bible helps us understand how this is meant to look, but how we hate this idea of roles! How we fight it and rail and scream against it!

God says, [78]

Husband, love for your wife! Lead her. Provide for her. Praise her. Cherish her. Sacrifice your own will and desires for her sake. *Lay down your very life for her.*

Wife, submit to your husband. Respect him. Follow him. Honor him. Bless him. *Come alongside him to be his strong helper.*

Little child, honor your parents. Listen to them. Respect them. Love them. *Obey them.*

Father, instruct your children carefully. Lead them. Love them. *Guide them.*

Mother, nurture your children. Know their hearts. Care for them. *Train them.*

Adult child, don't stop honoring your aging parents. Speak respectfully to them and of them. Serve them. *Care for them.*

Why do we resist all this?
We resist it because it's hard.

The truth is that every member within a family unit is called within their role to exercise self-restraint and self-sacrifice; to lay down a piece of themselves for the sake of another—all for the sake of love.

True love means sacrifice, and sacrifice hurts!

Before Adam and Eve sinned, yielding to one another in this beautiful, selfless way was easy; but the sin and selfishness residing in our hearts make laying down our own wills painful. The fact that our spouses, kids, and parents all too often don't deserve this kind of love, honor, and respect makes it even harder—they are sinners too. Yet God says, *do it anyway. Love, respect, and honor your family unconditionally.* We can only live this way with God's help; thankfully He stands by strong and ready to teach us His ways.

Family was designed by God to point us to Himself.

The beautiful institution of family was established to help us humans understand *who God is* and *what love is*—for God is love.[79] This modern idea of "family" we have created where each member is all and only for him or herself has nothing to do with God, and it knows nothing of His love. We discover our true selves not primarily for our own personal fulfillment, but so that we can lay our lives down for the sake of others.

And yet...*it is in laying our lives down for others that we discover the greatest and truest heights of personal fulfillment!*

I love what Dallas Willard writes about the Trinity:

> Each member of the Trinity points faithfully and selflessly to the other in a gracious, eternal circle of love...

> At the core of reality is the circle. It's the circle of Father, Son, and Spirit. The Son submits to the Father, and the Father loves to glorify the Son, and the Son is driven by the Spirit, and the Spirit reminds everybody of the Son. The Father also sends the Spirit, and there is an endless, eternal, humble, gentle—all those words that Paul wrote way back in Ephesians—community.

> That's the Trinity with one another. That's what's real. That's the most real thing in existence.[80]

Does that sound so terrible? No! It is breathtakingly beautiful! *It is true love in action.* Everyone gives of themselves, and everyone carries out their role. The end result is symmetry and harmony. The end result is that *everyone* is honored and lifted up!

When we mess with the image of the family, we not only cheat ourselves, our families, and our society; we also twist reality and mar the very image of Almighty God. Is it any wonder God's enemies are hell-bent on destroying the family?

So wives, let's go back to God's design! Let's submit to our husbands. Submission is not about being a weak doormat, that is just what the Lie tells us. Submission is being so incredibly strong with the strength of God and so secure in His love *that we don't have to be constantly proving ourselves*. Submission is having so much confidence in God *and* in the men we married that we don't have to always take control. It means trusting our husbands' ability to make decisions, too; and not needing to contradict and direct them at every turn.

Let's respect them! Willingly place ourselves under their leadership and protection. Tell them how much we admire and look up to them.

Husband, *love* and *serve* your wife. The love she needs doesn't come easily or naturally, so you have to learn. You have to study. *Listen* to her! *Praise* her! Be present with her. Lay down your own life and your dreams in order to provide and care for her. Step up and take charge of leading your family, leaning hard on God's wisdom and love.

Submitting ourselves to God's design leads to stability, peace, and beauty. Until we stomp on the cunning Lie that tells us otherwise, we will never discover the fullness God intends for our families.

Ordinary Sex: Anything But Ordinary

Physical intimacy is designed by God to be the heartbeat and life spring of a marriage relationship. Everything else flows out of these miraculous moments when a husband and wife are joined together physically, emotionally, and spiritually— all three at once. Sexual oneness between husband and wife is meant to be a further illustration of the miraculous love and oneness that exists in the Trinity.

The Bible teaches that sex is so much more than just the detached physical act our culture would have us believe it is. It is more than just an urge or instinct. More than a physical need.

Sex is holy.[81]
Ordinary living means reclaiming its place of holiness in our lives.

Sex is a gift for us to unwrap and enjoy to the full, but it is a sacred gift. We have to treat it with the greatest honor and care. We have to treat *each other* with the greatest honor and care. God designed love-making to be about connection, intimacy, and oneness...not *only* physical pleasure.

Our culture has desecrated sex in every possible way. We have trampled on it, ripped it up, strangled it, and dragged it through the mud.

Nothing could be more tragic and catastrophic to a civilization.

The Lie tells us it's just a physical act, and we believe the Lie. We gorge our eyes and our bodies on sensual pleasure but we ignore the cries and needs of our hearts and our souls. Then we wonder why deep down we are so lonely, isolated, and insecure—so starved for acceptance and love. There is another way!

The Lie tells us it's a private decision how we engage in sex; that it's no one else's business. But God says otherwise. He says it is *His* business, and that what we do in private affects not just ourselves; but our family, our society, and our world.

When we are starved of true love, we can't pass it on to anyone else around us.

America, God wants us to have amazing sex. The best sex ever! But amazing sex isn't chiseled bodies, hair extensions, plastic surgery, and "freedom" to "love" whomever or whatever whenever and in whatever ways we want.

The secret to sexual fulfillment is unconditional, committed, forever love between a husband and wife that is rooted in the love of Jesus Christ. *This* kind of love is rare and precious. It can only grow stronger, more fulfilling, and more enticing as time marches on. *More and more satisfying* even when hair begins to gray and skin starts sagging and bagging!

This kind of love really exists. We have to stop listening to the Lie! It is robbing us!

Nothing can compare to the rest, trust, acceptance, and joy that comes when a husband and wife know they have eyes *only for each other*...and no one else. When they can say with joy, "I belong to my beloved, and his desire is for me!" Song of Solomon 7:10

When we rip the deep emotional connection out of sex between man and wife—a connection which is cultivated over time as years pass and love matures—we cheat ourselves of one of the greatest treasures on earth. Don't let the Lie steal this extraordinary *ordinary* that could be yours.

"The strength of a nation lies in the homes of its people."

—ABRAHAM LINCOLN

13

ORDINARY LIVING...

WITH OUR CHILDREN

"Then God blessed them and said, 'Be fruitful and multiply...'" Genesis 1:28a

One of the most heart-breaking trickle-down effects of the lie of socialism (specifically all subversive attempts to *destroy the family*) is our society's diminished regard for children. More and more, children are regarded as optional and they are seen as expendable. If babies show up in our lives at a time that is inconvenient for us, we can literally just kill them. *And this is normal.*

If and when children *are* brought into the world in this country, they are often kept at arm's length. Children are increasingly viewed by our culture at large as annoying little interruptions. They are pushed as far off to the side as possible by their parents. We may *say* we love our kids, but the truth of our actions show that we moms and dads of America are far too busy and preoccupied with bigger and better things than to bother with the monumental task of loving, training, and shaping the hearts of our children.

The Bible teaches presents a radically different view of kids. It says children are a blessing from God! A reward! *They are priceless treasures.* "Children are a gift from the Lord; they are a reward from Him." Psalm 127:3 Living ordinary according to

God's design means accepting the high calling of parenthood *and rediscovering its joy*.

The Hearts of Fathers and Children

The very last two verses written in the Old Testament are powerful and often overlooked. If you were writing the Bible, how would *you* draw the entire first half of the Bible to a close?

God says,

> Look, I am sending you the prophet Elijah before the great and dreadful day of the Lord arrives. His preaching will *turn the hearts of fathers to their children, and the hearts of children to their fathers.* Otherwise I will come and strike the land with a curse. Malachi 4:5, 6

This is how God chooses to wrap up the entirety of His Old Testament. *This* is the word God leaves hanging in the air through the 500 years of silence between Malachi and the start of the New Testament!

Take note, world! There is a prophet coming to prepare the way for Jesus' coming. And what will his preaching do? His preaching will turn the hearts of fathers to their children, and the hearts of children to their fathers.

Sure enough, a page flip and 500 years later, the first person we meet in the New Testament is the prophet John the Baptist. This is precisely the message he preached:

Repent! Repent! Turn away from sin and turn back to God! Dad, this means turning your hearts toward your kids! Kids, this means turning your hearts toward your dad.[82]

It is astounding that God pairs *repenting* (turning our hearts away from sin and back to God) with *turning our hearts toward our children*.

We must not miss the weight of what God is communicating through these verses. The word is specifically directed toward fathers, and that is important to note. Dads, this is first and foremost on you. But it also applies to mothers; and I believe grandparents, too.

Dads, is there something keeping you from turning your hearts toward your kids?

Career? Success? Money? Friends? Entertainment? Leisure? Sports? *Ministry?*

If your heart is not turned toward your children, your heart is not turned toward God.

Family is that important.

Moms, where are *your* hearts directed? Have you ever made a conscious choice to turn your heart toward the hearts of your children? Their hearts are open and reaching for a connection! If your heart is not open and available to them now, to what or whom will they attach their hearts?

Grandparents, have you ever truly turned your hearts toward your grown sons and daughters? Are you interested in listening to them, connecting with them, and knowing who they are? Do you take seriously your role in passing on your faith and values down to your grandchildren?

Turning our hearts toward our children is both a one-time decision *and* a moment-by-moment decision. It is choosing daily to be present, available, and interested in our children as precious and important people. It is choosing to be fully dialed-in on the mission of loving them, training them, and raising them up to be God-fearing members of society.

God confronted me personally with this truth one evening several years ago. I will never forget that night. During a retreat of solitude, God pierced my soul and showed me that even though I was a "full-time mom," my heart was not turned toward my children. I loved them, of course. I was taking good care of their needs. *But my heart wasn't pointing primarily in their direction.* My heart was pointing outward, away from my family, toward other work and other ministry.

The slow turning around of my heart was painful and difficult. It was humbling. It was like trying to turn a giant ocean liner that had been sailing full-steam in the opposite direction. The reversal was awkward and slow, but I wouldn't turn back now for the world. Embracing motherhood in this heart-dedicated way has led to so much joy and a deep sense of purpose. A deeper connection with my children has also begun to grow, which is more valuable than gold.

Turning our hearts toward our children will play itself out differently in different families. For me as a mom, it led to me to laying aside a visible ministry to embrace a hidden ministry in my home. It meant moving the bulk of my writing time to the early hours of the morning so I could be available for my family when they were awake. It meant ditching the distraction of social media so I could be more present in my home. It meant getting down on the floor more often to play with my kids; curling up with more picture books on the couch; listening more carefully to their thoughts and ideas; celebrating more vivaciously the beauty of their stick-man art; and slowly building up a discipline of daily pointing their souls to God's Word...daily speaking *out loud* the wonders of God's goodness and faithfulness. For my husband and me, turning our hearts toward our children also led to us taking an active rather than passive role in their education.

What would it look like for you to turn your heart toward your children?

Ordinary Child-Rearing

If the connection between the hearts of parents and their children is so critically important to God, it is no wonder the socialist agenda makes a priority of separating children from their parents. The *destruction of the family* has always been a key component of socialism.

Some time ago I stumbled on a post in a socialist forum on Reddit that caught my attention; it gives startling insight into why this is.

> The destruction of the family does not mean that people will be taken away from their parents or anything. It means that the families' role in capitalism is a micro way of reproducing and promoting social values and skills for the next generation of workers. To [accomplish] this it is necessary for the family to run the household and be responsible for childcare.
>
> In communism, the families' work will be placed upon the community. Childcare, food preparation, cleaning, and whatever else...will be moved from the family. It will no longer serve as the basis for capitalism to continue.[83]

Socialists recognize the immense power of *ordinary family life*. And—this is shocking—what this socialist is specifically recognizing here is the power of *homemaking!*

Homemaking is a threat to socialism!

What?!

Karl Marx wrote, "Thus, for instance, once the earthly family is discovered to be the secret of the holy family, the former must itself be annihilated theoretically and practically."[84]

The modern democratic socialist movement has not violently taken our kids away from us (at least not yet), but it has succeeded in separating them from us subversively. Today in America, most of our young children are raised by daycare workers, public school teachers, and after-school program directors. Forget universal healthcare; "universal preschool" is one of the latest and greatest promises in campaign speeches today.

The problem is not that there are not wonderful teachers and daycare workers out there; there are. It is just a bald fact that the earlier and more completely children are separated from their parents, the less their hearts and minds are going to soak up the ideology *of their parents*.

Socialists acknowledge that childcare, cooking, cleaning—all the mundane, everyday activities that Americans have grown to despise—are the *very avenues* by which a society passes on its core beliefs to the next generation.

It is time for the rest of us to realize this, too!

Cooking, cleaning, making cookies, taking out the trash, raking the lawn, weeding the garden, tackling house projects, playing together, eating together, praying together...these are not meaningless tasks but rich opportunities through which—over time—we pass our values down to our kids. It is through repetitive, intentional, everyday life that they soak up the meaning of family and love, the value of hard work, and the importance of serving one another. This is how they learn practical life skills and leadership lessons, learn to give expression to creativity, and so much more.

If socialists see that the most effective way to stop Christian values from being passed on from one generation to the next is to get someone—anyone!—else besides mom to complete the tasks of a homemaker, *could it be that the most effective way to keep those values alive would be for mom to step back into her job as homemaker again?*

The answer is yes! *Yes!*

Moms, don't underestimate or undervalue the world-shaking power of your *ordinary!*

With the financial pressures facing so many of us today it might feel like an impossibility for mom to stay at home, but if there is anything I have learned in 35 years of walking with God it's that when we take a step—even a small, faltering step—to align our lives with God's design, He opens up a way to help us. He provides!

For mom to forego or reduce her income might require some serious sacrifices. It might mean living in a smaller house, making do with one car, moving to a cheaper neighborhood, living in a less-desirable part of the country, letting go of some luxuries, and—perhaps most challenging of all—giving up the accolades of society. But moms, *what if? What if we went back home?*

What if we dedicated the biggest portion of our hearts, intellect, education, and talents to the world-shaking task of *raising a secure, loved, and well-trained generation for the glory of God?*

Our society will never be saved by a surge of triumphant women rising and crashing through the glass ceiling.

No.

This culture will be healed by an army of *extraordinary, ordinary mothers lovingly getting down on their hands and knees to clean up broken glasses of spilled milk.*

C.S. Lewis writes,

> I think I can understand that feeling about a housewife's work being like that of Sisyphus (who was the stone rolling gentleman).[85] But it is surely in reality the most important work in the world. What do ships, railways, mines, cars, government etc. exist for except that people may be fed, warm and safe in their own homes? ...your job [homemaking] is the one for which all others exist.[86]

If the homemaker disappears from our society, America, *what do we have left?*

Education Matters

I have here next to me a reprint of *The New England Primer*[87]— the first textbook printed in colonial America. It was originally printed in the late 1600s and was used by families and teachers to teach letters and reading even into the 1900s. It was widely used for over 240 years! For over 150 years it was *the* primary textbook used to teach American schoolchildren how to read.

In this country, we often discuss how America was founded upon Christian principles, but it is astounding to see with my own eyes what was taught to American schoolchildren back then. *The New England Primer* is not just a book of ABCs. *It is a solid and thorough book of theology.* Here are some tiny excerpts:

A wise son maketh a glad father, but a foolish son is the heaviness of his mother.

Better is a little with the fear of the Lord, than great treasure & trouble therewith.

Come unto Christ all ye that labor and he will give you rest.

Do not the abominable thing which I hate saith the Lord.

Except a man be born again, he cannot see the kingdom of God.

A In Adam's Fall we sinned all.

B Heaven to find, the Bible mind.

C Christ crucify'd, for sinners dy'd. [88]

For most of America's history, it was *ordinary* for American children to grow up knowing who God is. Not all of these kids ended up with a personal relationship with Jesus, of course; but the children of this country grew up under the basic assumption that God exists. They were taught what He is like and how He designed human beings to live. This knowledge about God was as foundational to them as learning their ABCs!

This, my friends, is the most precious *ordinary* of all that our culture has lost. *Our children do not know who God is.* And as a result, they don't know who they are, either.

Moms and Dads, ensuring that our children grow up with a solid view of the world that *begins and ends with God* is our responsibility. No one else's. This morning in my daily Bible reading I came to Matthew 18, and I believe there is a strong word here for parents today. It begins,

> Jesus called a little child to him and put the child among them...

Picture your son or daughter standing in front of Jesus; or a grandchild, niece, or nephew.

> ...Anyone who welcomes a little child like this on my behalf is welcoming Me. But if you cause one of these little ones who trusts in Me to fall into sin, it would be better for you to have a large millstone tied around your neck and be drowned in the depths of the sea. Beware that you don't look down on any of these little ones. Matthew 18:2, 5-6, 10a

This world is pushing viciously, ferociously hard to win over the hearts and minds of our kids. *We have to push back harder.* Providing a God-centered worldview for our children is not a luxury for some parents who are blessed with an abundance of time and resources; it is a command for all parents who fear God.

For some parents, this might mean making a sacrifice of time and space to homeschool. For other parents, this might mean making a sacrifice of money to send their kids to a good Christian school. For still other parents, it might mean sacrificing the energy it takes to get inside the public schools and help their kids separate Truth from the Lie inside those walls.

Whatever battle strategy we choose, we have to accept the fact that fighting for the hearts and minds of our children in this culture today *is a real battle.*

If we are not fighting the battle, we are losing the battle.

So commit yourselves wholeheartedly to these words of mine. Tie them to your hands and wear them on your forehead as reminders. Teach them to your children. Talk about them when you are at home and when you are on the road, when you are going to bed and when you are getting up. Deuteronomy 11:18, 19

These verses in Deuteronomy show us that introducing our children to God is to be a day-in, day-out, all-encompassing mission. God's primary method of spreading the Good News of Jesus Christ throughout the world is through *ordinary family life!* Through *generations!* To be a parent or a grandparent, an aunt or an uncle, is to be a missionary. Whatever we have been given in terms of faith and knowledge of God, *this is what we are required to pass on to our kids*.

What our kids choose to do with this knowledge when they grow up is up to them, but as long as they are under our rooves it is our job to set them up as best we can to know Jesus Christ and to view all of this world and all of life through the crystal clear lens of Truth.

"If only it were all so simple! If only there were evil people somewhere insidiously committing evil deeds, and it were necessary only to separate them from the rest of us and destroy them. But the line dividing good and evil cuts through the heart of every human being. And who is willing to destroy a piece of his own heart?"

—ALEKSANDR I. SOLZHENITSYN

14

ORDINARY LIVING...

AMONG OUR NEIGHBORS

"Now the man and his wife were both naked, but they felt no shame." Genesis 2:25

This verse is an original picture not only of perfect love within a marriage but also of perfect unity within humanity. In Genesis, Adam and Eve's perfect unity—marked by complete vulnerability and absence of shame—was broken when sin entered into the human heart.

As soon as the first marriage was marred by human sin, all hope for world peace was tragically, sorrowfully lost until the day when Jesus Himself will come back to restore it. Perfect love was broken and unity went up in flames.

How God must have wept that day! He could see the pain and suffering this was going to mean for every generation to follow. He could see, even then, the hurt and tragedy this brokenness would cause our generation right here in the United States today.

Love and unity cannot be restored to the earth *in full* until Jesus returns, but something begins to happen as we turn our own lives over to Jesus Christ, and as we then allow Him to start rebuilding and healing our broken families. The more we allow the power of His Truth to change our personal, ordinary lives within our own homes, the more His Truth and love begins to flow powerfully outward! His healing overflows to touch our neighbors, our friends, our communities, and our society!

God's love has great power to alter the course of this world even in its Fallen and sinful state.

But for this to happen, we have to do something radical. We have to adopt *God's ordinary* not only within our families but also when it comes to the way we interact with our neighbors.

Even though it feels today like our nation has been turned upside down and the entire world is going mad, God's ordinary command to *love our neighbors as ourselves* hasn't changed. His ordinary command to *love our enemies* still stands.

The million-dollar question is this: What does it mean *to love them?*

~∞~

Socialism has its own special version of love.

Socialism tells us that to prove our love *for* this neighbor we need to *hate, fear,* and *label* that neighbor. To prove our love for one neighbor, we need to take part in judging the motives of another neighbor. We need to live in suspicion of that other neighbor. We need to monitor his every move. We need to publicly shame him if he appears to stray. We need to silence him.

This kind of "love" does not lead to unity. It leads to further hurt, division, and chaos.

This is not by accident, but by design. Marx teaches that in order for socialists to reach their goal of replacing capitalism with socialism, they first have to divide society into antagonistic groups.

Socialist activists have been working hard for years to make entire groups of Americans look like enemies in each other's eyes, using the strategy of "raising class consciousness." As discussed previously, this is a fundamental Marxist tactic used by activists to incite class struggle and also to create a group think/group act mentality so people can be swayed more easily in a certain direction. This may sound like a conspiracy theory, but it comes straight out of Marxist textbooks. NYU Professor Ollman writes,

> For the individual, class consciousness is not so much something they have or do not have as it is something they give expression to or participate in when in a group along with other workers, when acting and thinking in their capacity as group members dealing with the situation and problems that are peculiar to the group. At these times, the people in the group both perceive what is taking place (which includes how they hear the questions of the researcher) and respond to it (intellectually, emotionally, and practically) differently than each individual does or would on his own.

> Changes of mind, in particular, are strongly affected by the group. For example, in a group that is moving in one direction, it is easier for the individual, given some degree of identification with the group, to change his mind in the same direction than it would be if he were on his own.[89]

One of the main reasons such deep and divisive chasms have opened up between groups of American citizens in recent years is because socialists have been busy creating collectives. I believe one of President Obama's most significant accomplishments in his eight years in office was the extent to which he *raised class consciousness* in this country. By the time he stepped down from his political office, we all had a label. We were all part of one well-defined collective or another.

Socialism defines all human beings as either part of an *oppressor collective* or an *oppressed collective*. For example,

> All white citizens today must wear a label that says, "OPPRESSOR." All black citizens and those of other minority groups must wear a label that reads, "OPPRESSED."

All men must wear a label that says, "OPPRESSOR." All women must wear the label, "OPPRESSED."

Anyone whose beliefs state that marriage is for one man and one woman must wear the label, "OPPRESSOR." Anyone in the LGBT community: "OPPRESSED."

A law-abiding citizen: "OPPRESSOR." An illegal immigrant: "OPPRESSED."

Defenders of the U.S. Constitution and individual rights: "OPPRESSORS." Progressives whose collectivist dreams are inhibited by the Constitution: "OPPRESSED."

The 1%: "OPPRESSORS." Everyone else: "OPPRESSED."

Socialism's Litmus Test of Love

Socialists tell us that the ultimate way to prove our love for our neighbor and to free everyone from the stigma and pain of their collective class labels is to support *real change.*

Institutional change. *Systemic* change.

But what does that actually mean?

It means that if we *really* love our (collective) neighbor, we must support socialism.

This is especially evident right now in the realm of racial justice. It is important for Americans to understand that race is being intentionally leveraged by activists to garner public support for socialism. Julia Wallace and Jimena Vergara, in their article *Black Liberation and the Early Communist Movement* recently published by *Left Voice,* explain how rising racial tensions in the United States today are directly connected with the great struggle for socialism. They write,

> The only way to end systemic racism is to end capitalism, and the only way to lead a powerful movement against capitalism

is to root out the racism that still prevails in large sections of the working class...

We believe that Black liberation is at the heart of class struggle in America, and that the fight against racism should be at the center of a left organization's practice. ...To that end, we must use the legacy of socialists in the Black struggle to rebuild the relationship between Black liberation and Marxism as a new political and social force.[90]

Socialists tell us in no uncertain terms today that every white person in America is racist; and that America's entire history, its traditional values, and everything about our capitalist society have been poisoned by racism. They go on to tell us that the only way (the only way!) to rid ourselves of this racism that plagues all of American society is *to end capitalism, destroy all traditional American values and institutions, and implement socialism.*

The Truth About Systemic Racism

Racism, the belief that "race is the primary determinant of human traits and capacities and that racial differences produce an inherent superiority of a particular race,"[91] is a detestable evil wherever it exists in human hearts, and wherever it is exercised in thought, word, or action. *It is evil because it suppresses the Eternal Truth that all men have equal worth and value in the eyes of their loving Creator.*

Racism denies the Eternal Truth that every human life has dignity.

Racism is a sin.

Christians are always and forever called to oppose racism wherever it is proven to exist. We are also called to oppose unjust and discriminatory laws—as American abolitionists did in the Civil War, and as many citizens did in the fight to end segregation laws and to ensure African American citizens received the right to vote. Fighting racism is good and it is right.

The idea of *systemic* or *institutional racism*, however, is something altogether new and different. We hear the term being used everywhere today. What does it actually mean?

The term "institutional racism" was first coined by proponents of the Black Power movement in the 1960s.[92] Sociologist Professor Joe Feagin is more recently credited with developing "systemic racism" as a theory.[93] He unpacks the concept in his book *Systemic Racism: A Theory of Oppression*,[94] published in 2006.

Feagin describes systemic racism like this:

> I utilize "racial oppression" and "systemic racism" as shorthand terms for the European American oppression of African Americans since the 1600s. ...As I will show, this white-generated and white-maintained oppression is **far more than a matter of individual bigotry**, for it has been from the beginning a material, social, and ideological reality. For a long period now, white oppression of Americans of color has been **systemic—that is, it has been manifested in all major societal institutions**."[95] (emphasis mine)

The theory of systemic racism seeks to fundamentally change America's traditional (Judeo-Christian) definition of racism. It explores, explains, and addresses the problem of racism from a Marxist/materialist worldview and places it within a collective framework of justice.

Systemic racism is not primarily about changing specific laws that discriminate against minorities; Feagin admits that few such laws exist today: "most antiblack discrimination is no longer legal."[96] What it seeks to do is to bring an end to material imbalance (class struggle) and informal discrimination (alienation) between blacks (exploited) and whites (exploiter) through aggressive systemic change (revolution).

It believes, in accordance with the materialist teachings of Marx, that all of America's capitalist ideals, laws, systems, and institutions *grew out of* an economic base of slavery and were *created* primarily to maintain white domination over blacks. Thus, it equates the entire system of capitalism and all traditional American values and institutions with racism and seeks to overcome them through revolutionary class struggle and the implementation of socialism.

Marxism and Systemic Racism

The theory of systemic racism starts with Marx's false assumption that humanity's deepest, most basic problem is a material tug-of-war between oppressor and oppressed. Anyone who wishes to gain a true understanding of racism in America must, according to Feagin, start by taking a look at all of America's past and present through Marx's materialist oppressed/oppressor lens. Feagin writes,

> What is missing...is a full recognition of the big picture—the reality of this whole society being founded on, and firmly grounded in, oppression targeting African Americans. ...All racial-ethnic relationships and events, past and present, must be placed within that racial oppression context in order to be understood.[97]

Systemic racism also collectivizes guilt. No longer is racism to be considered an individual sin problem to be dealt with and addressed on an individual basis, as the Bible instructs. It is now considered to be a collective problem. It is a *white* problem that must be dealt with collectively:

"One important step in this racial reframing," Feagin explains, "is to get whites to recognize and name the racial 'problem' accurately. The problem of racism has always been, most centrally, a white problem."[98]

He goes on to say, "Most western analysts have viewed social justice in individualistic terms... We must go beyond individual conceptions of social justice to a group conception." [99]

And no individual white American can escape the weight of this collective guilt. The introduction to Feagin's book *Racist America: Roots, Current Realities, and Future Reparations* states: "Racism...is found not only in small pockets of society, but is practiced by all Americans, permeating the social fabric of our lives."[100]

The theory of systemic racism also aligns itself with Marx's belief that all distortions of human nature are the result of our social environment and our economic condition—not the result of sin in the human heart. All whites are racist, Feagin claims, because all American *systems* and *institutions* are inherently oppressive and are perpetuating this racism.

> For white-on-black oppression to persist across many generations since the 1600s, many millions of white individuals and groups have had to participate actively in the ongoing collective and discriminatory reproduction of the family, community, legal, political, economic, educational, and religious institutions that necessarily undergird this oppressive system.[101]

> Like a hologram, each apparently separate institution of this society—including the economy, politics, education, the family, religion, and the law—on closer examination still reflects in many ways the overarching reality of racial oppression.[102]

Feagin's theory assumes Karl Marx's conclusion that the only way "distortions of human nature," in this case racism, can be eradicated from society is through the destruction of capitalism by means of class struggle. Systemic racism necessitates the destruction of America as we know it. What we need, according to Feagin, is a radical cultural revolution and a complete overhaul in the way Americans view and experience family, religion, law, and politics. *What we need is socialism.* This stands in direct opposition to the Eternal Truth of God, which states that the Only Way humanity can improve is for one heart at a time to be made new through faith in the saving power of Jesus Christ.

Feagin lays out the following specific steps to cleanse America of systemic racism. When activists demand "real change" to end systemic racism, this is the kind of change they desire:

- Reconfigure the traditional patriarchal family structure.[103]

- Replace the U.S. Constitution and Bill of Rights with new founding documents.[104]

- Add a new Economic Bill of Rights which would include the human rights to food, clothing, recreation, and adequate medical care, among other things.[105]

- Eliminate all undemocratic elements of government such as the Senate and electoral college so we can have true democracy (instead of a republic).[106]

- Eliminate states' rights.[107]

- Reeducate white citizens so they can identify and eradicate their racism or "white racial frame" (defined as "an organized set of racialized ideas, stereotypes, emotions and inclinations to discriminate... which typically become part of an individual white consciousness at an early age and...often exists in individual minds at a nonreporting and unconscious level.")[108]

- Reform the educational system to equip teachers and children (from an early age) to identify and replace the "white frame."[109]

- Replace America's traditional conception of individual justice with a new framework that includes collective justice.[110]

- Implement large-scale reparations.[111]

- Institute economic socialism by redistributing wealth equally across society: "fair distribution of societal goods."[112]

- Reevaluate traditional foreign policy in order to partner more closely with the U.N. and other global groups who are working to eliminate systemic racial discrimination worldwide.[113]

- Outlaw hate speech.[114]

Throughout the book Feagin drops hints about where exactly within "the system" he believes "the problem" is embedded:

"Today, the Republican party is the omnipresent guardian of whiteness in this society."[115]

"The gun culture so distinctive of the United States today has roots in the violent enforcement of slavery by armed whites over two centuries."[116]

"Historically most white religious groups (mostly Christian) supported slavery...For centuries, white religious officials have been leaders in developing the ideology that rationalized slavery and subsequent societal oppression in more or less patriarchal terms." [117]

"The phrase..."family values" typically means white-determined values."[118]

Feagin leads us to assume that Conservative and Christian Americans are the guiltiest perpetrators of systemic racism because their beliefs support capitalism and protect traditional American values and institutions. By this assessment, we can fully expect that Christians and Conservatives would, under socialism, require the most vigorous reeducation to remove their deeply embedded "whiteness," or traditional beliefs and worldview.

Systemic Racism: A Master Deception

The theory of systemic racism takes many real and valid truths—like the truth that evil slavery and legal racial oppression existed in America's past, and the truth that many African Americans suffer the excruciating pain of prejudice today—and twists and weaves those truths together with socialist lies to create a confusing, deadly web of deception.

In 1942, Bonhoeffer wrote, of national socialism in Germany,

> This great masquerade of evil has played havoc with all our ethical concepts. For evil to appear disguised as light, charity, historical necessity, or social justice is quite bewildering to anyone brought up on our traditional ethical concepts, while for the Christian who bases his life on the Bible, it merely confirms the fundamental wickedness of evil.[119]

We need to up our guard against deceit today. Deception is flying at us from angles we never would have dreamed possible. Joining the fight against systemic racism appears on the surface to be the moral, loving, and right thing to do. However, when we dig a little deeper we find that the theory of system racism is not just anti-capitalism and anti-America; it is anti-justice, anti-family, anti-Christian, and anti-God.

Marxists have tried many times in the past to pit collectives against each other for the sake of social justice and equality, *but they have never one time in history succeeded*. All they have ever done is to create more poverty, hunger, division, and oppression. And guess who gets hit first and hardest with that poverty and hunger? *The very "exploited" class socialism promised to rescue.*

The Real Culprit: Systemic Socialism

Destroying capitalist America isn't going to help anyone. There are specific laws and policies in place today, however, that are harming citizens of all color in poor communities today. These policies are not *racist* policies; they are *socialist* policies.

In *The Problem with Socialism*, Thomas DiLorenzo has a whole chapter devoted to proving that welfare programs *harm* the poor and trap them in poverty rather than lifting them out. He writes,

> In the latter half of the twentieth century…private philanthropy was increasingly displaced by government programs, which were not only far more bureaucratic but far less effective than private charity had been. Traditional American private charities focused on helping people to help themselves. Government programs, inevitably, became much more focused on creating "clients" to justify the ever increasing number (and salaries) of bureaucrats. In the process, "compassion" no longer meant self-sacrifice for the benefit of others, but merely rhetorical support for more government welfare programs…[120]

He goes on to say,

> …from the 1950s until the 1960s, thanks to America's vigorous post-war economy, the number of people living in poverty had declined by about a third. But from 1968, as the

massive increase in welfare benefits began, to 1980, when Ronald Reagan was elected president, poverty increased by 22 percent..."Poverty" went up because "poverty" became attractive...welfare discouraged people from getting jobs, because the more money one earned the more one was likely to suffer reduced welfare payments, food stamps, housing subsidies, and other benefits...

Welfare programs have become an alternative to work. A 1992 study by economists Richard Vedder and Lowell Gallaway found that only 18 percent of welfare recipients moved out of poverty, compared to 45 percent of poor people who did not receive welfare.[121]

DiLorenzo lists minimum wage as another example of a socialist policy that hurts citizens in low-income neighborhoods,[122] and there are so many more we could list. Socialist policies do not uplift the poor; they suppress and hold them back.

Dream with me for a moment here. What if the government stepped out of the role of caring for the poor and removed all the overbearing regulations that slow down and limit non-profits? What if the government allowed the local church to work more freely among the poor again? I believe churches would absolutely jump at such an opportunity, and that we would begin to see a change in the landscape of America's cities. The gospel changes lives!

And what if Roe v. Wade were overturned? Roe v. Wade is one legal ruling that disproportionately hurts the African American community. African Americans only make up 13.4% of America's population, but 36% of babies aborted each year are African American.[123] This is almost identical to the number of white babies aborted even though white citizens make up 76.6% of the population![124] *Why are a higher percentage of black babies being aborted than white babies?* Just remember Margaret

Sanger's "pioneering" and "scientific" vision of a socialist utopia. If it weren't for Roe v. Wade, there would be over 21 million more African American lives in our country today. What a gift that would be for all of America! *We want more black lives in America!*

All socialism does by "raising class consciousness" is prey on the vulnerabilities of citizens who are enduring genuine hurt and hardships and use those hardships to manipulate the masses for the benefit of a small group of politicians who will ultimately gain political control. It is cruel, it is evil, and it is unjust.

God's Way of Love

So what is God's ordinary way for us to love our neighbor in these tumultuous times?

Real love must, first and foremost, always uphold Truth.[125]

Just as Satan's cruelty can be disguised as compassion, but in the end be deadly; so God's true Way of Love can initially appear to be tough, but in the end it always proves sweet. The God-fearing American today has the difficult, wildly unpopular, but critical job of both standing against true racism and unjust laws wherever they are proven to exist and also exposing the false teachings that are paramount to the theory of systemic racism.

Our culture is redefining sin, twisting God's standard of justice, and presenting America with false hope for healing. Christians cannot take part in this.

It is not right to join the mob in judging the intentions of people's hearts or making collective accusations against our neighbors. Judging the *hearts* and *motives* of our neighbors is something the Bible says only God can do (Jeremiah 17:9, Matthew 7:1-5, Luke 6:37). God tells us today,

You must not pass along false rumors. You must not cooperate with evil people by lying on the witness stand. You must not follow the crowd in doing wrong. When you are called to testify in a dispute, do not be swayed by the crowd to twist justice. And do not slant your testimony in favor of a person just because that person is poor. If you come upon your enemy's ox or donkey that has strayed away, take it back to its owner. If you see that the donkey of someone who hates you has collapsed under its load, do not walk by. Instead, stop and help. In a lawsuit, you must not deny justice to the poor. Be sure never to charge anyone falsely with evil. Have nothing to do with a false charge and do not put an innocent or honest person to death, for I will not acquit the guilty. Exodus 23:1-7

Embracing and spreading a materialist theory of class struggle and oppression is not love. The most loving thing we can do for our neighbors today is to point them in the direction of *God's amazing grace.*

There are elements of truth sprinkled all throughout the theory of systemic racism. All of human history and all of our present existence are, indeed, tainted. But they're not just tainted by racial prejudice—they're tainted by all kinds of sin. And contrary to Marxist thought, it is not only members of the "oppressing class" who own the potential for wrongdoing. The Bible teaches that every human being who has ever existed is capable of and guilty of sin.[126]

Sin is a heavy, real weight on human shoulders. Each and every one of us stands condemned. Everything good we try to do really is tarnished, stained, and worthless.

But there is good news! *God gives grace!*

By His grace, good things can be found all throughout history alongside evil things! Painful things can be transformed into beautiful things. Failures can be turned into opportunities. Sinful, fallen people can be used by God to accomplish His good plan for the world.

There is no hope for healing for our nation outside of Jesus, but with Jesus, there is true hope. We human beings are all guilty of sin, but we don't have to groan and stagger under the heavy burden of guilt any longer. In Jesus, there is complete forgiveness from sin. Through Jesus, we can forgive ourselves and we can forgive others, too.

I have a vivid memory from when I was very small, maybe 3 or 4 years old. I was sitting in the front pew of a tiny country Baptist church in Vermont with several other children. We kids were learning a song; and as we sang, the words swirled around and around in my little mind. They made an impression on me. They sank deep into my heart and took root there. The words of the song went like this:

Jesus loves the little children;
All the children of the world.
Red and yellow, black and white,
They are precious in His sight.
Jesus loves the little children of the world.

Jesus died for all the children;
All the children of the world.
Red and yellow, black and white,
They are precious in His sight.
Jesus died for all the children of the world.

Jesus rose for all the children;
All the children of the world.
Red and yellow, black and white,
They are precious in His sight.

Jesus rose for all the children of the world.[127]

The answer is really so simple. So simple that children understand it faster than we grownups do. The truth is, none of us have to sink under the heavy weight of socialism's "oppressed" and "oppressor" labels any longer. We can rip them off and throw them in the fire! Because every human being is born wearing the same label:

"**GUILTY** SINNER LOVED BY GOD."

When we meet Jesus, He mercifully takes care of the "guilty" part for us. His grace erases our guilt and adds a new word to our label forever. Our new label then reads,

"**FORGIVEN** SINNER LOVED BY GOD."

It's not that we no longer commit sin; because we do. It's that the *guilt, shame,* and *penalty* for our sin is wiped away and completely paid for by Jesus' death on the cross. It is finished! When Christ makes our hearts clean based on His goodness, not ours, this is what God says about us: "So now there is no condemnation for those who belong to Christ Jesus." Romans 8:1

The only way to break free from the guilt of our sin and the only way to be healed from the suffering and pain the sin of others has inflicted upon us is to *run to the cross of Jesus Christ.* God's grace changes everything.

We have freedom and permission and a command[128] from God to detach from the collective.

We can begin viewing ourselves and our neighbors as plain old regular individual human beings again. Human beings who are sinners. Human beings who desperately need to know they are loved by God. Human beings who are all part of one race: *the human race.*

"No man can be consistently both a Socialist and a Christian. It must be either the Socialist or the religious principle that is supreme, for the attempt to couple them equally betrays charlatanism or lack of thought."

—The Socialist Party of Great Britain

15

ORDINARY LIVING...

AS THE CHURCH

"When it was time for the harvest, Cain presented some of his crops as a gift to the Lord. Abel also brought a gift—the best portions of the firstborn lambs from his flock. The Lord accepted Abel and his gift, but he did not accept Cain and his gift. This made Cain very angry, and he looked dejected."
Genesis 4:3-5

In Genesis 4, we come upon a scene in which Cain and Abel, the grown sons of Adam and Eve, are offering sacrifices to God. From all outward appearances, both of these men appear to be doing something good and right. However, God is only pleased with one of their sacrifices. He accepts Abel's sacrifice but rejects Cain's. Why?

Hebrews 11:4 tells us that God accepted Abel's sacrifice because he offered it *in faith*. Abel was trusting in God's grace as his only hope of acceptance and forgiveness. His sacrifice was a demonstration and outpouring of his *faith*.

Cain, however, made a big mistake. He thought it was the religious act *itself* God wanted. But God is not interested in moral action that is divorced from true faith. The Bible teaches us that the only good works God ever accepts are those which flow out of sincere faith in the saving work of Jesus Christ on the cross:

> "For the Scriptures tell us, 'Abraham believed God, and God counted him as righteous because of his faith.'" Romans 4:3

> "For by grace you have been saved through faith; and that not of yourselves, it is the gift of God; not as a result of works, so that no one may boast." Ephesians 2:8, 9 (NASB)

God lovingly implored Cain to turn to Him in faith and warned him ahead of time what would happen if he didn't. God said,

> "Why are you so angry?" the Lord asked Cain. "Why do you look so dejected? You will be accepted if you do what is right. But if you refuse to do what is right, then watch out! Sin is crouching at the door, eager to control you. But you must subdue it and be its master." Genesis 4:6, 7

Tragically, Cain ignored God's warning. Instead of choosing faith, he hardened his heart even more, and as a result, he was overpowered by his sin. He wasn't able to control it! His anger toward God grew into a murderous rage directed at Abel. One day, Cain invited Abel out into a field and *murdered him in cold blood*.

Then, after the murder, Cain kept running from God. He ran as far away as he could and settled with his family in a land called Nod. There, we learn, his descendants multiplied and grew into a violent and corrupt society.[129]

This evil society began with a single religious sacrifice that was offered to God without true faith. It began with one man who placed his trust in the power of his own moral actions rather than believing "it is impossible to please God without faith." (Hebrews 11:6)

As darkness spreads and grows in our nation today, we God-fearing people have some soul-searching to do. Are *we* guilty of removing true faith in Jesus' work on the cross from our religious activity? Have we been trying to please God on the basis of our own moral actions?

If any of us have, God invites us back to faith! He warns us, just as he warned Cain: *Watch out! Sin is crouching at the door, eager to control you!*

"Be careful then, dear brothers and sisters. Make sure that your own hearts are not evil and unbelieving, turning you away from the living God." Hebrews 3:12

Ideological Subversion and the American Church

Socialist ideological subversion has infected nearly every aspect of American society. In this chapter, we ask a difficult question: *Has it affected the Church?* We are going to discover that it has—much more than many of us realize. Today, many "liberal" *and* "conservative" Christians are accepting Marxist ideas with open arms and mixing them with Christian theology. This mistake is altering the way many people understand the gospel and the mission of the Church. American Christians face an urgent need today to return to *God's ordinary plan for His Church.*

God loves His Church! The Church of Jesus Christ cannot be identified as a certain denomination worshiping in a specific way inside any one type of building. God's Church is made up of a myriad of diverse individuals from around the world—individuals who have, through faith, accepted Jesus Christ as their Savior. The Bible says God gives these believers new, clean hearts;[130] and that He seals their souls for eternity by giving them the gift of the Holy Spirit.[131]

Together, all people who have put their faith in Jesus Christ as their only hope of salvation comprise God's true Church.

The Church is imperfect in its current state. Both individually and corporately, the Church is in the process of being molded and prepared for the future Kingdom. But even in its imperfect state, it is precious and beautiful. The Church is no exclusive club. Its door stands wide open to every individual willing to believe that Jesus Christ is the only answer to man's deepest problem: sin.

Within the true Church, all members hold equal worth and importance. To be rich or poor, male or female, black or white, Taiwanese or Uruguayan, educated or uneducated, tall or short, fat or skinny, young or old, doesn't affect anyone's value in the least. The Church is the only true great leveler of humanity. It is literally God's adopted *family*, and our heavenly Father never plays favorites.[132]

The Church is also described in the Bible as the "Body of Christ." I Corinthians 12 teaches that Christ is the head of this spiritual Body and that every single individual member is equipped with a special gift from the Holy Spirit meant to benefit the rest of the Body. Every member of the Body is necessary for the health and vibrant beauty of the whole.

The Church is unified and made one not because of members' special ability to get along well, or because of any human effort, but because they are bound together spiritually in the person of Jesus Christ through the Holy Spirit.

While the Church is a universal family that exists beyond walls, buildings, and borders, it is also an institution that exists within local communities. This is not an either/or phenomenon, but a both/and reality. God established the institution of the local church, just as He established the institutions of family and government, to fulfill a specific purpose on earth. The local church, under the headship of Christ, provides order, leadership, and accountability for the Body, and it helps spread the Good News of the Kingdom of God.

When Jesus comes back, there will be no more need for temporary earthly institutions, but for now, our lives as the universal Body of Christ are meant to be lived out and expressed both personally *and* within the context of a local assembly of believers or "church." The institution of the local church is a gift from God.

Socialism, however, has always sought to destroy it. Today it does so subversively.

The Social Gospel

The most obvious way that socialist ideology has influenced the American church is by convincing many Christians that socialism is not only *compatible* with Christianity, it *is* Christianity—in fact, it is the purest expression of Christianity we can live out in this world. All across America, the Christian gospel of salvation by grace through faith alone is slowly being displaced by a new gospel: the social gospel.

In November 2019, *Christianity Today* published an article titled, *Does Socialism Have to Be 'Godless'?*[133] in which contributing writer Heath Carter gives a rave review of a new book by Vanessa Cook. In her work *Spiritual Socialists: Religion and the American Left*,[134] Cook provides us with an overview of the 1900s rise of the American social gospel, or what she calls "spiritual socialism," and points to it as an example for America's "religious left" to follow.

Early proponents of this movement (she mentions activists like Felix Adler, Staughton Lynd, and Peter Maurin) sought ways to soften the violent edges of 20th-century communism and make socialism more palatable for religious people who had been scared off by its previous horrific failures. Spiritual socialists, according to Cook, helped form the present-day democratic socialist vision of a "non-violent" form of Marxism.

These social gospelers also helped expand traditional Marxism, which focuses exclusively on labor relations, into the "cultural" or "Neo"-Marxism of today which applies Marxist theories of oppression to other areas of society as well:

> No longer tied exclusively to Marxism or the "labor metaphysic," as C. Wright Mills would later call it, spiritual socialists addressed the whole person as a sacred agent of God. Accordingly, issues of oppression were extended to include race and gender and state-sponsored violence, in addition to class. The spiritual socialist vision made progress on these fronts (in fact, on all fronts of oppression) a theological and practical necessity. In other words, the only way to cultivate the Kingdom of God was through careful attention to root, structural problems that obstructed human dignity and harmony in any way...

> More specifically, spiritual socialists envisioned a future, utopian society that reflected the teachings and practices of Jesus. They believed that the Kingdom of God on earth, when brought to full fruition, would be a society of perfect peace, cooperation, and equality among all persons. This amounted to their spiritual interpretation of socialism, another word they used to describe the Kingdom come.[135]

In other words, they made Marxist ideas necessary tools for establishing God's Kingdom on earth. Cook celebrates 20th-century spiritual socialists as heroes of the faith, but a close observer will see that their "faith" appears to be in the essential goodness of humanity, not in the saving work of Jesus Christ. Cook writes,

> [Spiritual socialists] did not all advocate absolute pacifism, but they did believe, contrary to conservative evangelists like Billy Graham and Christian realists such as Reinhold Niebuhr, that human virtues and moral values could reshape international relations and redeem a sinful world.[136]

The social gospel ignores the reality of a sin nature and believes, with Marx, that to improve humanity all we have to do is change economic and social systems. The social gospel retains basic Judeo/Christian morals and may uphold Jesus Christ as an inspirational religious figurehead, but it quietly rejects major biblical doctrines and removes Jesus as *Savior of the world*. It presents another way for humanity to reach God's Kingdom: socialism.

> Though he rejected religious dogma and doctrine...Adler retained Reformed Judaism's emphasis on moral duty, social justice, holy community, and the eschatological Kingdom of God. ...He conceptualized a pluralistic idea of God, a manifold "universe of spiritual beings infinite interacting in infinite harmony."[137]

> Lynd wrote of a "common religious experience that different persons might use quite different words to describe." A faith in the "inner light" or spiritual potential of every human being, acting in concert toward common ideals, also undergirded Lynd's defense of democracy: "We need each other because none of us can see the whole truth."[138]

> For Lynd...it became clear that the central message of Christ, in his preferential option for the poor and his moral resistance to the prevailing order, was a sort of democratic socialism based on religious values. "Jesus's program," Lynd wrote in an essay years later, "was empowerment from the bottom up, to rebuild peasant dignity and hope without waiting for God to do it."[139]

> "Be what you want others to be," Maurin exhorted. ...To give and not take, this is what makes men human." Such mundane acts, he believed, were the measures of our humanity and the makings "of a new heaven and a new earth, wherein justice dwells." Such was Maurin's vague notion of the Kingdom of God on earth, a society in which "all men would be able to

fulfill themselves" and feed themselves; he spoke of a society in which "it is easier for people to be good."[140]

Cook doesn't seem to have any issues with this kind of theology. She lifts up these 20th-century pioneers of today's social justice movement as an inspiration. She writes,

> They showed that socialism need not be secularized, narrowly political, or godless and un-American. They also illustrated that religion was not inherently conservative or purely personal, but also progressive and collective. ...Spiritual socialists, by bridging the secular and religious, the individual and collective, recognized that finding common ground politically meant finding common ground spiritually, even among outright atheists.[141]

That last sentence is telling and accurate. If Christians want to become socialists, they have to stretch the boundaries of Christianity and move beyond their core Christian beliefs. They have to compromise. *Because socialism and the true gospel of Jesus Christ are fundamentally and diametrically opposed.*

The social gospel, being resurrected as the "social justice movement," is a false gospel. Marxism, already itself a counterfeit Christianity, has simply cloaked itself with moral language and Christian terms to make it more appealing to a "religious" society. And it's working. In his article for *Christianity Today*, Carter praises Cook for the "tremendous service" she has done for us by "lifting up a spiritual-socialist tradition that has languished too long in obscurity."[142] He writes,

> Little wonder that, fully 30 years after the fall of the Berlin Wall, so many American believers struggle to conceive of the possibility that anything good could come of socialism. The remarkable witness of the radical Christians at the heart of this book suggests otherwise. Their faith moved mountains. The least we can do is expand our moral imaginations.[143]

Christians, beware. Democratic socialism is quickly replacing Christianity as America's religion of choice, and it invites us to come along for the ride. All we have to do, along the way, is *deny the power of the old rugged cross*.

Socialist activists have been working for years to alter America's understanding of justice and the true mission of the Church. Today, many even within the evangelical world are openly requesting their insight. In 2015, democratic socialist Bernie Sanders was invited to give a convocation speech to a cheering crowd of students at Liberty University, an historically conservative evangelical Christian university in Virginia. In his speech, Sanders admonished students if they believed in the Golden Rule and truly cared about issues of justice and morality, to search their hearts and ask themselves whether they should join the democratic socialists' moral struggle against *wealth inequality*.[144]

In 2019, the Southern Baptist Convention (SBC) voted to adopt a resolution embracing critical race theory and intersectionality (popular social philosophies built squarely on the theories of Marx) as "analytical tools" that may be "employed" by Christian leaders "to address social dynamics."[145] Some pastors at the convention voiced serious objections to this resolution, but it was still passed by a large majority.

An organization called Founders Ministries released a documentary called *By What Standard? God's World...God's Rules*,[146] recounting the story of how the largest conservative evangelical denomination in America came to adopt a resolution that validates Marxist ideology. The film explains critical race theory and intersectionality for those who are not familiar with those terms and shows how they fundamentally oppose not just minor but major, foundational teachings of the Bible.

The documentary serves as a wake-up call for believers and exposes just how widespread the influence of Marxism is becoming within the evangelical church. I encourage every Christian to watch Founders Ministries' film. It can be viewed for free online at www.founders.org/cinedoc/.

The True Mission of the Church

There is grave danger in confusing the mission of democratic socialism with the mission of God's Church. Many people living in Jesus' day missed His coming because they were looking for a human leader who would establish a new social order right then and there. *Jesus didn't come to do that.* He came first to solve the spiritual problem of individual sin. The Kingdom He planted is, in its present form, a *spiritual* Kingdom:

> "Jesus answered, 'My Kingdom is not an earthly kingdom. If it were, my followers would fight to keep me from being handed over to the Jewish leaders. But my Kingdom is not of this world.'" John 18:36

Many American Christians, sadly, have grown impatient with Jesus. He's taking too long to establish His Kingdom. Socialists are taking action *now*. Socialists promise to perfect humanity and end poverty *today*.

But it can't be done, because we all still have sin natures.

God absolutely cares about our physical well-being. He tells His Church to care for widows and orphans. To have compassion on the poor. To speak for the oppressed. To be generous when we encounter people in need—especially those within the faith. To give and give more and then to keep on giving. The Bible tells us that Christians are to treat everyone equally and never to show partiality. We are to value, respect, and honor the poor just as highly as we do the rich; and the rich just as highly as we do the poor. These are all vital, integral parts of being the hands and feet of Jesus on this earth.

However, we are never instructed anywhere to "take down" the rich or create a classless society. Both Paul and Peter actually admonish slaves to "submit to their masters."[147] These verses do not in any way condone or excuse the sinfulness of slavery as some have erroneously claimed they do, but they do illustrate clearly that Marxist class struggle is not God's mission for His Church or His chosen method for establishing the Kingdom.

We are also never instructed to take *someone else's* money or property away from them for the sake of the poor. As we have established before, God calls this theft, not justice.

And while Jesus tells believers to pursue peace with everyone,[148] He also tells us explicitly that the gospel is not about creating world peace or a harmonious social order. He says,

> "Don't imagine that I came to bring peace to the earth! I came not to bring peace, but a sword. 'I have come to set a man against his father, a daughter against her mother, and a daughter-in-law against her mother-in-law. Your enemies will be right in your own household.'" Matthew 10:34-36

The Church's true mission is to build God's *spiritual Kingdom* by pointing sinful, hurting people to the cross of Jesus Christ. Our mission is to make disciples by teaching believers how ordinary life in God's Kingdom is meant to be lived. The Church is instructed to watch and wait with patient faith and enduring hope for the glorious return of King Jesus, who at just the right time will return to establish a physical Kingdom of peace and perfect justice on earth.

> "Then the seventh angel blew his trumpet, and there were loud voices shouting in heaven: 'The world has now become the Kingdom of our Lord and of his Christ, and he will reign forever and ever.'" Revelation 11:15

While social and material change is never the primary goal of the gospel, the glorious truth is that it is often a present, tangible, and beautiful result of the gospel. So many families and communities around the world, through Jesus, have been freed from the shackles of hatred and prejudice! So many have escaped poverty! But the true wealth of God's Kingdom can't be seen or touched in its present form. It is immaterial. It is found in the person of Jesus Christ Himself, and in the love that exists within His true Church. It consists of an abundance of hidden spiritual treasures that far outweigh any material possessions we could own on earth. *This is something the unbelieving world around us can't comprehend.*

Local Church: Back to Ordinary

God is building His spiritual Kingdom right now. It continues to spread and grow like wildfire around the world today within the hearts of His people. But there is another kingdom, a kingdom of darkness, that is constantly trying to thwart God's Kingdom. "And from the time John the Baptist began preaching until now, the Kingdom of Heaven has been forcefully advancing, and violent people are attacking it." Matthew 11:10

We, the Church of America, must shake ourselves awake. We are being tested and tried. False teaching abounds, and not enough Christian leaders are stepping up to the critical task of helping their flocks separate truth from lies. Now COVID-19 has brought rattling lock-down restrictions, face mask orders, and church closures. I know of many believers who are feeling lonely, lost, and disconnected. Some of us experienced deep sadness when we realized "watching church" online during COVID-19 wasn't all that different from "watching church" in person from the pew. We all know the local church was never something we were just supposed to *watch*; it is a vibrant, essential part of Christianity we long to *live*.

What are we supposed to do when we face sad, real, and increasing discrepancies between what we are experiencing within the local church and what we know from the Bible is supposed to be occurring there?

The answer isn't to give up. God says,

> Let us hold fast the confession of our hope without wavering, for he who promised is faithful. And let us consider how to stir up one another to love and good works, not neglecting to meet together, as is the habit of some, but encouraging one another, and all the more as you see the Day drawing near. Hebrews 10:23-25 (ESV)

We believers need to cling to one another now more than we ever have before.

It may be tempting in troubled times to attack and destroy the entire institution of the church, but that isn't the right answer. Destroying the institution is what socialism would tell us to do! We don't have to ditch church today; we just need to return to God's intended design for the church. Here are some glimpses at what God's *ordinary* looks like for the institution of the church:

- Local churches look to Christ as the ruling Head of the Church—not to the government or any other leader. (Ephesians 1:22; 4:15, 16; 5:23; Colossians 1:18)

- A plurality of male elders/bishops acts as spiritual shepherds, overseers, and teachers under the direct headship of Christ. (I Timothy 3, Titus 1)

- Godly shepherds teach sound doctrine and speak God's Truth boldly and unapologetically. They actively protect their flocks from false teaching and lies. (Matthew 7:15; 2 Peter 3:17; 2 Timothy 1:14; Titus 1:9, 2:10)

- A plurality of male (and arguably female—Romans 16:1) deacons serve and address practical needs within the church. (I Timothy 3)

- Christians pray together regularly! (Acts 1:14, Acts 2:42, Acts 12:12)

- Churches observe the ordinances of the Lord's Supper and Baptism. (Matthew 26, I Corinthians 11, Matthew 28:19, Romans 6:3-5)

- All members exercise their spiritual gifts with joy for the benefit of the Body. (I Corinthians 12, Ephesians 4:11-16)

- Church life includes intergenerational fellowship. Generations need each other! (Psalm 145:4, Titus 2:3-5)

- Shepherding and discipleship are relational in nature; they include both teaching and personal example. (John 10:3-5, 14, 15; 13:1-5, 34, 35; I Peter 5:3; 2 Timothy 2:2; Titus 2:7)

- Hospitality is an important and wonderful part of church life. Christians share meals and gather together often in one another's homes. (John 21:9-15; Acts 2:46)

- Believers stir one another up to love and good works. (Hebrews 10:24)

If you are part of a solid, vibrant church, praise God! Cherish it, and continue using your gifts to serve your local body.

If you are a Christian who, for one reason or another, is without a local church home right now, however, I want to encourage you. *God sees you. He knows.*

What if He wants to do something new?

Do not forsake the assembling of yourselves together! Try to find a good church, but if you can't find one, know that there are other displaced Christians also searching for the Body right now. Pray for God to bring other likeminded believers into your life. Seek them out! Invite them into your home to eat and to pray.

Ask God to revive His Church, and ask Him to begin with you.

If you are a godly man who meets the qualifications of elders,[149] ask God if there is a possibility He might want you to take this a step further. Pray about seeking other godly men who also meet the qualifications of elders and starting small, intimate church gatherings in homes or elsewhere.

Do whatever it takes to find ways to assemble together for worship and to seek the Lord as a Body according to His ordinary design. We need each other today more than ever. *We need the church.*

The End of Times and the Apostate Church

The Bible says that before Christ returns, there will be a great "apostasy," or a great falling away from the Truth. "Let no one in any way deceive you, for it [the return of Jesus] will not come unless the apostasy comes first, and the man of lawlessness is revealed, the son of destruction." 2 Thessalonians 2:3

Apostasy is a threat within the church and a real temptation for Christians today. America is full of people who have had complete access to the Truth of God and yet are intentionally walking away from Jesus. By God's grace, let us not be found in those ranks.

Dear Christian, do not grow weary while doing good. Do not grow impatient while you're waiting for Jesus. "At just the right time we will reap a harvest of blessing if we don't give up." Galatians 6:9

"So I saw that there is nothing better for people than to be happy in their work. That is why we are here!"

—Ecclesiastes 3:22

"Diligent hands will rule, but laziness ends in forced labor."

—Proverbs 12:24 (NIV)

16

ORDINARY LIVING...

AT WORK

"The Lord God placed the man in the Garden of Eden to tend and watch over it." Genesis 2:15

Adam, without ever having to lift a finger, enters the world with a crystal clear *identity*. He is *human*: the most glorious creation of Almighty God, set apart from the rest of creation because he alone is the image-bearer of God.

God is a God who *works:* He designed the universe! He formed it, cares for it, rules over it, and sustains it. As His image-bearer, Adam received the high privilege of sharing in the joy and deep fulfillment of God's *labor*. Work is, therefore, *good*. Completing his God-given work assignment brought deep fulfillment to Adam and great glory to God.

Understanding God's design for work has the power to change everything about our ordinary workday. We, too, are created beings. Each one of us, man and woman, are made special and unique *in the image of God*. Without ever having to lift a finger, we arrive on this earth *valuable* and *loved* because we are valuable to God and He loves us.[150]

We also arrive carefully designed and equipped *for a unique work assignment*. There is deep meaning embedded in our labor when we submit our work to God. God has a job for us to do!

He has a job for me to complete on this earth, and He has a job for you as well.[151]

Our sinful, fallen nature has marred our clear identity as God's image-bearers and has stolen our true purpose away from us. *But both of these things are restored when we meet Jesus.* His work on the cross pays the price to bring our true identity *and* our meaningful work assignment back.

Our everyday labor—physical and/or mental labor—becomes the miraculous and ordinary avenue through which we express our God-given identity and serve Almighty God. Any and all labor—scrubbing floors, building a house, preaching a sermon, feeding a horse, designing a website, changing a diaper, researching an article, delivering mail, you name it—becomes a potential offering that can be lifted up to God in love, infused with His power, and used to accomplish His good purpose on this earth.

In God's economy, there is great dignity and deep potential meaning to be found in *all labor*. God says, "Whatever you do in word or deed, do all in the name of the Lord Jesus, giving thanks through him to God the Father." Colossians 3:17

Socialism's View of Labor

Socialism approaches the subject of work from a different angle.

Mick Brooks, a contributing writer for *Marxist.com*, helps us understand the beliefs supporting socialism's view of labor. He writes, "What differentiates humans from other animals? We find that humans differentiate themselves by transforming themselves and external nature. The process by which people define and redefine themselves is the labor process."[152]

Socialists believe human beings have no unique identity outside of the work they do. When it comes to man's identity, socialism begins with a void.

Man doesn't know who he is!

After grasping at straws, man comes to the conclusion that it must be his *work* that sets him apart from the animal world; it is *work* that gives him an identity. Work is the only thing that makes a human different from a cow.

Work, therefore, becomes a god to him.

Work becomes *everything*; because *what a man does* defines *who he is*. Man has no value or worth apart from his work.

Linking work with man's identity in this way puts a lot of pressure on labor.

What does it say about who I am if all I do is push papers in a cubicle all day long? Who am I if the only job I can land is bagging groceries? Changing diapers is oppressive! It holds me back from proving who I am as a human being! I can't display my true value if I don't get that promotion. If I work all my days on an assembly line in a factory without recognition, who am I? It's not fair! It's unjust! Stop the oppression! I deserve more! *I demand something better!*

Work is plagued by futility, dissatisfaction, envy, and fear.

Socialists believe it is capitalism that is keeping them from reaching fulfillment in work, but sin is the problem, and Jesus is the only Road to true fulfillment in labor. Without Him, work really is just meaningless drudgery. It is grasping for the wind.

The Problem of Scarcity

The Bible teaches that ordinary work has dignity and that it can be filled with deep meaning and purpose through Christ. But let's be honest—it isn't all fun and games. There is a harsh reality on this earth that we all have to face:

Work is hard.

Economist Tom Rose writes, "Nature is...stingy...Man must work by the sweat of his brow even to eke out a bare existence for himself and his family, not to mention the many luxuries he might dream of enjoying."[153]

Economists call the basic problem all laborers face the problem of *scarcity*, and scarcity is an important concept to explore in any discussion of socialism, capitalism, and human labor.

Scarcity is really another word for *limitations*. Time, money, resources, strength, and talent are all limited here on earth. Because of scarcity, we human beings have to make choices. We have to make decisions. *Every day.*

We constantly have to choose *this* over *that*—what we will buy, how we will spend our time, with which occupation we will be employed. Often in order to get something we need, we have to let go of something we want.

Not all scarcity is bad. In the beginning, even before sin scarred the earth, man still had limits. He still had the responsibility of making choices.

For one thing, man was placed within the limits of time.[154] God had created day and night; so even in the Garden Adam and Eve had to make choices about what they were going to do when. Man was also given the limit of God's Law. Adam and Eve could eat from any tree in the garden…any tree *except one.*

Even in Paradise man faced limitations in his work, *because man is not God!*

So scarcity itself is not evil; it's just the opposite. Understanding scarcity helps us see our need for God.

Extreme scarcity, however, was never meant to be. Extreme scarcity is a direct result of the admittance of sin into the human heart. Before Adam and Eve sinned, their work environment was one of ease and plenty. They were never in danger of cold or hunger; they had all they needed and so much more.

Extreme scarcity exists on this earth because humans did not want to accept the limitations God had placed on them.

Adam and Eve rebelled. They ate the forbidden fruit. After they sinned, God told Adam,

> The ground is cursed because of you. All your life you will struggle to scratch a living from it. It will grow thorns and thistles for you, though you will eat of its grains. By the sweat of your brow will you have food to eat until you return to the ground from which you were made. Genesis 3:17b-19a

This harsh, unforgiving brand of scarcity is a result of the curse of sin on the world and is an inescapable reality of human life. Until Jesus returns, the Bible tells us that work will be a struggle. Making a living will be tough. Nature and evil will war against us. The dangers of poverty and hunger will continue to exist.

Socialism's "Solution" for the Problem of Scarcity

For Marx, the idea of *scarcity* was all rolled up in his theories of class struggle and alienation. He viewed scarcity purely as an *institutional* problem (created by capitalism) that could be remedied with *material* solutions (spreading the wealth).

Socialists don't believe in a sin nature. They don't believe in a curse on the ground. They don't believe in human limitations. They erroneously believe, therefore, that the economic problem of scarcity can be eliminated and eradicated from society.

If prices are controlled by the government so everyone can afford what they need, if division of labor is destroyed so no one gets stuck in a job that doesn't feel fulfilling to them, if everyone gets the same income from the government so no one has to live in poverty...humanity will shake itself free from the fetters of scarcity! Work will become easier and a lot more fun! We won't have so many difficult choices and frustrating limitations holding us back. We can *all* have our "bread...and roses too" as the socialist slogan promises.[155]

Dana Cooper, in another Marxist.com article, explains,

Under socialism, the line between the necessary labor we need to do to cover our basic needs, and the labor we do to realize ourselves as humans—often referred to as "hobbies"—would melt into each other. With more free time to pursue our real passions and interests, and with more and more menial, repetitive jobs automated through advances in technology, labor would lose the ugly character and connotations it has under capitalism. Under socialism you could work on an organic farm, help cure cancer, help develop an industry that does not destroy the environment, and play a concert—all in the same day! Not only would workers be part of projects that include everybody, they would make a tangible difference at their job every day, they would be fully realized members of society, and work to make it better, more efficient, and more fun.[156]

Under socialism, I can work on an organic farm, help cure cancer, help develop an industry that does not destroy the environment, and play a concert—all on the same day? Because my "basic needs" are provided by the government!

From a biblical standpoint, this is ludicrous. It is a hallucination that completely denies the reality of scarcity and also implies *that we are all the same;* that we have no unique design or special giftedness or personal work assignment from God. Ignoring the reality of scarcity and diminishing the beauty of human diversity in this way is evil, anti-God, and inhumane.

Economist Gary North writes,

"Marx was an escapist; he wanted to flee from time, scarcity, and earthly limitations. His economic analysis was directed at this world, and therefore totally critical; his hopes for the future were utopian, unrealistic, and in the last analysis, religious."[157]

If the Bible teaches that eradicating scarcity is impossible, what *actually* happens to scarcity when humans try to overcome it through socialism?

History has plenty of examples to share with us.

Scarcity, under socialism, *is magnified*. It is *unleashed*. It grows immensely *worse*. Hunger, poverty, and desperation in labor *spreads*.

Under socialist regimes, an overarching guiding Rule of Law is abolished, and this means citizens are no longer allowed to play by the same rules of the game in their daily fight against scarcity. Their hands are tied.

Because their earnings belong to the "collective," citizens lose the most powerful weapon they own in the battle against scarcity: *the sweat of their own brow. Hard work* is no longer rewarded. They lose their ability to *save* to protect their families against hard times and they lose any extra resources they might have had to *give* to help others hit with hard times.

If you want to have any chance of survival under socialism; if you want to attain any level of relief from poverty, honest hard work gets you nowhere. Instead what you have to do is comply with the government's demands and do whatever it takes to please government officials.

Soviet Communist Leon Trotsky explained socialism's true relationship with scarcity eloquently: "In a country where the sole employer is the State, opposition means death by slow starvation. The old principle: who does not work shall not eat, has been replaced by a new one: who does not obey shall not eat."[158]

God's Solution for the Problem of Scarcity

Socialism seeks to eradicate scarcity from society, but God says that's not possible on this side of heaven. He gives humans other methods for dealing with scarcity. He offers both practical instruction and supernatural assistance to help us deal with the problem of *extreme* scarcity on this earth.

What is a biblical response to the inescapable reality of scarcity?

Luke 16 holds a poignant and seldom-taught parable in which Jesus rebukes Christians for their lack of savviness and intentionality when it comes to the use of their earthly wealth and resources. Back in the 1700s, evangelist John Wesley preached a challenging and immensely practical sermon called *The Use of Money*[159] which was based on this parable. In his sermon, John Wesley outlines God's direction for the proper use of money in this way:

1) Gain all you can.
2) Save all you can.
3) Give all you can.

This is truly a wonderful summary of God's practical advice to humans for dealing with the problem of scarcity, and it just so happens that these three biblical directives *form a solid foundation for the economic system of capitalism*. Let's take a brief look at each of these commands.

1. Gain All You Can[160]

When John Wesley teaches the biblical concept of "gain all you can" he isn't talking about *greed* or *the love of money*, both of which are clear sins. He also doesn't mean overwork or workaholism—also sins.[161] He is emphasizing *hard work* and *smart investment*. This includes both physical and mental work.

God-fearing people are to be *hard-working* people. Just because we are a spiritual people with our sights are set on heaven doesn't mean we aren't called to live with our two feet firmly planted on this ground. God tells us to stop complaining[162] about how hard our lives are and *get to work*—but not on our own! *With the strength He provides!*[163] He also tells us to use the brains He gave us to make smart and profitable business decisions. This is good and right. It glorifies God!

Throughout Scripture, hard work and wise investment of earthly resources are celebrated, while laziness and wastefulness are condemned. *Hard work* is meant to be our number one weapon against extreme scarcity, and the Bible teaches that *true oppression* occurs wherever the rewards of an individual's hard work are stolen away from him.[164]

2. Save All You Can[165]

The aim of "gaining all we can," for the Christian, is never to spend it as fast as we can to promote our own vanity and elevate our own comfort.

Thrift is a long-lost *art of ordinary* that we Americans need to bring back to life! Jesus teaches us to live simply. To live within our means. To *live below our means.* To save money.

Saving money, in a very practical way, helps protect our families when extreme scarcity hits. It helps us survive when hard times come. *Saving money* also enables us to move on to command #3, which is most important of all.

3. Give All You Can[166]

Our saving is never all about us. We don't save to hoard up money for ourselves. We are called to *give our money away.* To give away *all we can!* Our money can be used by God to help *others* who are taken down by hard times, too! This is an important part of His plan for dealing with scarcity on earth. It is our responsibility, as the hands and feet of Jesus, to help others who are hungry and in need whenever we can. We are called to give not through force or guilt; but freely, generously, and joyfully! We are called to give out of pure hearts of love.[167]

God says that whenever we give our money away, we are investing it in a bank account where it will never be lost and it will never fade away. Whatever money we waste on ourselves here on earth is gone forever, but when we give our money away we are investing it in eternity.

For those who love God and honor Him through their everyday labor and earthly resources, there is even more good news. God also promises supernatural help in our fight against extreme scarcity. God's help is always near to His children—to those who are living and working not ultimately for this life, but for eternity.

God doesn't promise that our work will be easy, but He promises to lend us His own strength, guidance, and wisdom in our work *whenever we ask for it!* (Deuteronomy 8:17; I Chronicles 16:11; 2 Chronicles 16:9; Psalm 28:7; Psalm 37:17; Proverbs 3:5, 6; James 1:5; I Peter 4:11.)

God doesn't promise wealth or riches, but for those who seek His Kingdom above all else, He does promise to *provide for our basic earthly needs.* (Nehemiah 9:21, Proverbs 10:3, Luke 12:27-31, 2 Corinthians 9:8, Philippians 4:19.)

God doesn't promise worldly success or recognition for our work in this life, but He does promise that *He sees our work* and *He will reward* all the toil we do out of pure love and obedience to Him. (Genesis 16:13, Psalm 17:14, Psalm 58:11, Proverbs 27:18, Isaiah 40:10, Isaiah 49:4, Matthew 6:1, Matthew 24:46, Ephesians 6:7, 8; Revelation 22:12.)

Hard work, smart investment, earning rewards for one's labor, saving, and giving are all biblical commands that are strangled and stifled under the economic system of socialism. Capitalism, however, gives them a chance to flourish.

Slavery and Extreme Scarcity are Knocking on Our Door

Capitalism cannot and does not promise to eradicate scarcity from society, but nowhere else in the world have more individuals ever overcome the problem of extreme scarcity to the extent that we have under capitalism here in the United States of America. Nowhere else have more individuals owned such freedom to pursue God's *good and ordinary design for their work*.

But now socialists want to bring this to an end. They want to push taxes and regulations to new heights and they are pushing hard for a universal basic income. This is not the road to equality; it's the road to slavery. It opens the door wide for extreme scarcity to attack us.

America, don't let the Lie that says we can rid our society of scarcity deceive you! Don't let laziness and greed entice you!

Please don't trade away your priceless inheritance of *freedom* for a murky bowl of government stew...and captivity.

"Climate struggle is class struggle: the fight for socialism in our lifetime."

—JOHN PETERSON,
SOCIALISTREVOLUTION.ORG

17

ORDINARY LIVING...

ON PLANET EARTH

"God blessed them; and God said to them, "Be fruitful and multiply, and fill the earth, and subdue it; and rule over the fish of the sea and over the birds of the sky and over every living thing that moves on the earth." Genesis 1:28 (NASB)

The "climate crisis" movement continues to gain ground in the United States and around the world. Socialists have been tirelessly fighting to impose a sweeping piece of "emergency legislation" called the *Green New Deal* to address the "grave threat posed by climate change."[168]

This November 2019 article from *The Guardian* provides a good summary of what we are being told concerning the current state of planet Earth's climate, and how we should respond:

> The world's people face "untold suffering due to the climate crisis" unless there are major transformations to global society, according to a stark warning from more than 11,000 scientists.
>
> > "We declare clearly and unequivocally that planet Earth is facing a climate emergency...The climate crisis has arrived and is accelerating faster than most scientists

expected. It is more severe than anticipated, threatening natural ecosystems and the fate of humanity."

...They set out a series of urgently needed actions:

- Use energy far more efficiently and apply strong carbon taxes to cut fossil fuel use

- Stabilize global population—currently growing by 200,000 people a day—using ethical approaches such as longer education for girls

- End the destruction of nature and restore forests and mangroves to absorb CO_2

- Eat mostly plants and less meat, and reduce food waste

- Shift economic goals away from GDP growth

..."The good news is that such transformative change, with social and economic justice for all [aka socialism], promises far greater human well-being than does business as usual," the scientists said.[169]

Progressive socialists are telling us today that to overcome this grave "climate crisis" threatening life on earth we need to do three things: 1) reverse the earth's population growth, 2) fear our environment, and 3) submit to the demands of all living things.

These are the exact opposite of the commands *God gives us* in Genesis 1:28 about how we are to interact with our environment here on planet Earth.

God's Design for Humans and Their Environment

In Genesis 1:28 God gives us three clear instructions when it comes to rightly caring for our planet. He says: 1) fill the earth, 2) subdue it, and 3) rule over every living thing.

1. Fill the Earth

Population control, increasingly front and center in socialism's environmental agenda, is never God's answer to any world problem.

Never.

God explicitly commands man and woman to *fill the earth*. This is mankind's most basic calling, duty, and joy! More children being brought into this world is always a cause for celebration. In God's economy, new human life—and an abundance of it—is always welcome; it is always good. Anyone who says otherwise is violating God's Eternal Law and breaking far away from *His ordinary*.

In the article I quoted above, "longer education for girls" is listed as an "ethical" means of population control. This is highly offensive to me as a woman. Just as "women's rights" was a cover for population control in the days of Margaret Sanger, "women's rights" movement today is still being used as a means to achieve that end. Women, socialism isn't concerned at all with making us smarter; it's concerned with holding us back from our most important work *and decreasing the world's population*. Since when did it become "ethical" to manipulate women?

One of the most alarming responses I have seen to the "climate crisis" narrative is the growing trend of young millennials to go on "birth strike," pledging childlessness to help save the earth.[170] It is heartbreaking enough that these young people will never experience the wonder of parenthood...the sweetness of their child's first smile, the joy of walking her through each new stage of development. But it's even worse than that. They are committing familial suicide, purposefully ending their family lines.

Throughout history, pagan societies have created various idols that require sacrifices to protect humanity from nature. In the Old Testament, we read about the god Molech whose head was shaped like that of a bull. To appease him and to call forth rain, parents would lay their children down on Molech's altar and watch them burn alive.

Today's environmentalist movement is a modern spin on paganism that plays right into socialism's demand for ritual sacrifice.[171] Environmentalism is not about caring for our planet—it goes far beyond that. It is about worshiping "mother nature." It is about giving her whatever sacrifices she demands.

2. Subdue the Earth

Human beings are commanded by God not only to fill the earth but also to *subdue* it. Subdue is a strong word. It means t*o conquer. Tame. Overcome. Cultivate. Bring into subjection.*

This means that the earth was created to serve human beings; *human beings were not created to serve the earth.*

God places humans in a position of authority over all the rest of creation. We have a higher position than all animals! We are far more important than the fish and the trees!

It is evil and oppressive to place restrictions on human beings that God never placed on us. There is an entire laundry list of moral rules environmentalists would like us to follow, and today's anti-meat advocacy is a popular example of this. It is not immoral or environmentally irresponsible for humans to eat meat. God clearly stated otherwise to Noah after the Great Flood:

> All the animals of the earth, all the birds of the sky, all the small animals that scurry along the ground, and all the fish in the sea will look on you with fear and terror. I have placed them in your power. I have given them to you for food, just as I have given you grain and vegetables. Genesis 9:2, 3

3. Rule Over Every Living Thing

God's third instruction in Genesis 1:28 is closely connected with the second. God tells humans point blank that they are to *rule over* every living thing.

Fear and guilt are the primary motivating forces behind the climate crisis movement. Nothing could be further removed from God's command to rule over every living thing. Does God want us to use natural resources wisely? Of course! Does He want us to trash and abuse the earth? Of course not! However, making environmental decisions based on terror and nagging guilt does not fit with God's command for mankind to powerfully and authoritatively "rule the earth."

God is the only One who can teach us how to rightly care for our environment and to be good stewards of the resources He has provided for us. Taking the best care of our earthly home begins with an acknowledgment and respect for the God who created it.[172] *Otherwise, we will only end up harming the earth and harming fellow humans.*

The first step in rightly caring for our environment is fearing Father God, not mother earth. Mother earth is a demanding and cruel false idol. The Creator and Sustainer of heaven and earth is the God of love! He is the God who frees mankind from all our fears. He wipes away guilt and teaches us how to tend the earth in a way that will benefit both the earth He spoke into being *and* mankind.

Socialism and Climate Change

How closely tied is the climate crisis movement with the democratic socialist movement in the United States? They are one and the same! A writer for *Socialist Revolution* explains,

> The class struggle, in essence, is the struggle between and within the exploiting and exploited classes over natural

resources and socially produced wealth. When there is not enough to go around, people will fight over what is available...

A rational plan of production, distribution, and exchange, in harmony with the environment, is the only way forward for our species. Only a planned economy [socialism!] can mobilize the resources necessary to mitigate the effects of climate change. But you cannot plan what you do not control. The only way to assert control over the means of production is through ownership. Since the capitalists privately own the key levers of the economy, they make all the real decisions affecting the climate. Such a transfer of property from one class to another can only come about through revolutionary means.

The climate is already in revolt. Now it's up to the workers and youth of the world to rise up to bring down the entire system [of capitalism].[173]

Socialists have latched onto a false scientific problem and are using it to manipulate the masses. They have portrayed the emergency as dire and ratcheted up fear, especially among young people. As we see in the quote above, they have also provided us with a solution—the one and only solution that can create a sustainable future and rescue the climate for generations to come—indeed, the same solution that stands ready to solve all our greatest problems: *Destroy capitalism and replace it with socialism. Revolution!*

We need to carefully divide fact from fiction in the current climate crisis narrative and turn back to God's *ordinary* when it comes to our view of the environment and man's responsibility within it.

The Botched Science Behind Climate Change

How harmful *are* carbon dioxide (CO_2) emissions? Are we really causing catastrophic climate change every time we use fossil fuels such as coal, oil, and natural gas?

It turns out that the "scientific" data propping up the climate change crisis and hysteria comes exclusively from studies completed by one entity: the United Nations' Intergovernmental Panel on Climate Change (IPCC). The IPCC's studies are said to prove that human use of fossil fuels is responsible for climate change and is quickly leading us all toward global disaster.

Although the United Nations' powers-that-be want to convince us that the "science" of climate change is "settled," many independent scientists *outside* the intergovernmental panel have arrived at polar opposite conclusions through their own separate studies.

The IPCC's findings are based on computer models, and many scientists believe these models are flawed. C. D. Idso and K. E. Idso, from The Center for the Study of Carbon Dioxide and Global Change, cite, "inadequate computer climate models are the sources of multiple environmental misperceptions."[174]

After all the wildly inaccurate estimates that came from computer models during the COVID-19 crisis can we not all agree that making major national and world decisions based purely on computer model predictions is 1) not reliable and 2) not "science"?

Idso and Idso go on to state, astonishingly: "Science tells us that putting more CO_2 in the air would actually be *good* for the planet"![175] They explain,

> In the case of the biospheric benefits of atmospheric CO_2 enrichment, it is an indisputable fact that carbon dioxide is one of the basic building blocks of life, comprising the major "food" of nearly all plants on earth. With more CO_2 in the air, literally thousands of experiments have proven, beyond

any doubt, that plants grow bigger and better in almost every conceivable way, and they do it more efficiently, with respect to the availability of important natural resources, and more effectively, in the face of various environmental constraints. And when plants benefit, so do all of the animals that depend upon them for their sustenance, including us humans.[176]

A group of independent scientists and scholars have formed another panel called the Nongovernmental International Panel on Climate Change (NIPCC).[177] I was interested to read what this group with no government or United Nations affiliations would say about climate change. Here is what I learned:

While the NIPCC does not dispute the basic observation that some climate change is *occurring* (as it has continuously and cyclically all throughout history), they disagree with the IPCC's "foregone" conclusion that climate change is man-made. The NIPCC has published an 880-page scientific rebuttal to the IPCC report on climate change, providing substantial evidence to the contrary. This well-documented report (as well as shorter summaries of the report) are available for free to the public. I encourage everyone to check it out at *climatchangereconsidered. org*.[178]

In its report, the NIPCC maintains that "No close correlation exists between temperature variation over the past 150 years and human-related CO2 emissions."[179] It demonstrates and concludes that the net impact of burning fossil fuels is actually *beneficial* to both the environment and human health.[180]

Green Socialism Has Already Failed

The Green Energy movement in the United States is already a bust. Its "advances" are not real; they are an illusion. Green Energy is a living, breathing, current example illustrating the fact that socialism only and ever delivers hypocrisy, gross inefficiency, and destruction.

Michael Moore's 2019 documentary *Planet of the Humans*[181] illustrates this fact indisputably. It proves that:

1. Wind and solar energy are a pipedream. They are not only unreliable, inefficient, and inadequate sources of energy for widespread use; but the production and disposal of solar panels, wind turbines, and lithium batteries produce more toxic waste and do more harm to the planet than just using fossil fuels!

2. Most of the government (aka socialist) (aka taxpayer) money given to "Green Energy" projects has been completely wasted on building giant biomass (tree-burning) plants which produce just as much if not more pollution as fossil fuel plants *and also destroy our forests!*

As *Planet of the Humans* illustrates, billions of U.S. taxpayer dollars have already been flushed down the Green Energy toilet. The government-initiated and funded Green Energy movement has created more problems for our planet than it solves and is proving *itself* to be a living threat both to our environment and to human life and health.

Are other sources of energy besides oil a possibility for the future? Absolutely! Anything is possible. If we are serious about finding them, however, the government must stop subsidizing and regulating energy. The free market needs to be allowed to explore and test on its own what energy possibilities are actually efficient, sustainable, and economically feasible.

At the End of the Green Energy Rainbow

It turns out that the true motivation behind the global push to reduce $CO2$ emissions is not in truth a concern for our planet or concern for human life. It is much more sinister than that, and it is two-fold. The first motivation of the Climate Change movement is simply this: to gain control over people.

Socialist control.

Mark Hendrickson notes in an article for *Forbes*,

> If you control power, you control people…Who would lose if governments gain the power to order a significant reduction in CO2 emissions? Around the world, millions of people at the margins of survival would die. It would be a dispersed holocaust. Millions of others would suffer unnecessary impoverishment and deprivation. Even in wealthier countries, people who are affluent enough to afford the monetary costs could find their lives heavily regimented by government bureaucrats monitoring and limiting how many miles they may travel and what activities they may undertake.[182]

This is bad enough, but it gets even worse. Michael Moore's documentary *Planet of the Humans*,[183] which I mentioned earlier, tells us exactly where the Climate Change movement is taking us.

Michael Moore is an outspoken socialist, and the film stuns with its bare, honest, and candid assessment of what the socialist Left really believes when it comes to the Energy Crisis.

The film reaches its climax when narrator Gibbs, a lifelong environmentalist and Green Energy activist, comes to the shattering realization that "Green Energy," the movement to which he has devoted his entire life, is nothing more than an illusion, a myth, and a dream. That it is not actually doing anything at all to help save the earth and humanity from all its dire problems; and that it is, in fact, doing more harm than good.

"We humans are poised for a fall from an unimaginable height," he says. "Why, for most of my life, have I fallen for the illusion Green Energy would save us?"[184]

To help process this illusion-crushing revelation, Gibbs takes viewers along with him to visit social psychologist Sheldon Solomon of Skidmore College.

In Solomon's office, we watch Gibbs come to a full epiphany. He realizes Green Energy is not based on fact, science, and logic like he always believed it was; it is actually a *religion*. A socially-constructed set of beliefs our society has constructed to buffer ourselves from ever having to face *our fear of death!*

Gibbs says incredulously, leaning forward,

> "The Right has religion. ...Our side says, 'Oh, it's gonna be okay. We're gonna have solar panels. We're gonna have wind towers. As soon as I heard you talk about our denial of death I'm like...*could that be it? Could it be that we can't face our own mortality? Could we have a religion that we're unaware of?!*"

And Solomon replies, with a chuckle,

> "Absolutely! I think you've hit the proverbial nail on the head..."

Gibbs's mind is blown. He processes out loud,

> "What I'm hearing is that if I haven't come to grips about my own anxiety about death and life, and am presented with a reminder of that, I'm highly likely to make some tragic decisions for the community."

Solomon answers,

> "Yes."[185]

The documentary uncovers example after example of how it is an *underlying fear of death* that has caused America to waste billions of dollars on energy alternatives that don't work, aren't cost-effective, and aren't actually sustainable. If you haven't watched the film, please do. It is a must-see.

Jeff Gibbs comes to a crisis moment in his belief system—a moment where he could turn away from the empty promises of socialism and reach for God. But he doesn't. Instead, he takes the only next logical step forward within the construct of the Lie. Psychologist Sheldon Solomon brings their searching discussion to a close with these words:

> The only solution in principle is, you know—as Albert Camus put it, he said, "There's only one liberty to come to terms with: *death*. Thereafter, anything is possible." I find that downright inspiring![186]

The only final solution humanity can reach on its own, when it is truly honest about the insurmountable problems it faces, is to embrace the nothingness; to embrace the absurdity of life; and finally, *to embrace death*.

Moore and Gibbs boldly and chillingly forecast what lies in the future for America if we continue to welcome the religion of socialism with open arms instead of turning to Jesus. In the film, they ask, "Can a single species that's come to dominate an entire planet...be smart enough to voluntarily limit our own presence?"[187] And anthropologist Steven Churchill warns, "Without seeing some sort of major die-off in population there's no turning back."

Only human sacrifice can save us now.

We glimpse here the real purpose of climate change and the ultimate end goal of socialism. Its bloodthirsty fangs are even now baring their teeth in America just as Shafarevich[188] told us they would. *The true end of the socialist rainbow is the death of humanity.*

My fellow Americans, you are indeed free to fully embrace and become one with death if you want to. You absolutely have that freedom. Just know that if you do, that is exactly what you will get: *death*. Death forever and ever and ever.

Not ultimate liberty, but everlasting chains.[189] Not victory, but utter despair and loneliness[190]...terror and torment[191]... *weeping and gnashing of teeth.*[192]

There is a better option!

Jesus Christ, the Son of God, is the only One who could overcome death by meeting it head-on and embracing it. At this moment in history, we don't have to blindly follow the path of death. We can choose the Path of Life![193]

"There is no other rule or test for who is a member of the people of God or of the church of Christ than this: where there is a little band of those who accept this word of the Lord, teach it purely and confess against those who persecute it, and for that reason suffer what is their due."

—MARTIN LUTHER

18

RESIST!

JOIN "THE ACTIVE STRUGGLE AGAINST EVIL"

"Submit yourselves therefore to God. Resist the devil, and he will flee from you." James 4:7

We have learned a lot on this journey. We know now that socialism is an age-old movement that has surfaced again and again in societies around the world all throughout history. Socialism is a counterfeit Christianity that seeks to right the wrongs of the world *without the help of God*. It is anti-God and anti-individual, and its ultimate goal is the death of humanity.

This all-out war against God and individualism always includes, in one form or another, the abolition of private property, the abolition of the family, the abolition of religion, and communality or equality.

The brand of socialism growing in popularity in America today is called democratic socialism; it takes the core beliefs and theories of Karl Marx and gives them a modern social and moral spin. Democratic socialists seek to eliminate poverty and create a new civilization marked by social and material equality and environmental consciousness. Democratic socialism seeks to govern society through "democracy" which in truth would lead to crippling bureaucratic regulation and oppression.

Democratic socialism views capitalism as inherently exploitative based on the antiquated and long-disproved labor theory of value. To cleanse our society of this so-called capitalist exploitation, socialists believe they must destroy capitalism and fundamentally change all traditional American social institutions. While socialist revolutions of the 20th century were primarily revolutions of violence, the Democratic Socialist Revolution of America has up to this point been a revolution of ideological subversion.

Today we have reached a critical point in history when Americans must decide whether or not we are going to surrender our rights and liberties to socialism.

Submit Yourselves to God

The battle against socialism is first and foremost spiritual. James 4:7 (*"Submit yourselves therefore to God. Resist the devil, and he will flee from you."*) tells us that the power to push back evil arises from ordinary hearts and ordinary lives that are humble before God. That's why we just spent six chapters exploring God's ordinary design for human beings. If we truly want American freedom to last one more day, if we want our lives to make a difference for good in this nation, the first step is to get down on our knees and submit our lives to God's ordinary design.

Today is the day to lay down our own lofty ideas about how human life is meant to be lived and our thoughts about how the universe is meant to be run. There is a Truth that stands higher than human wisdom. Surrender to it! Surrender to *Him!*

Truth has a name: it's Jesus!

Then...and only then...will we have the strength it takes to take decisive action based on the authority and power of God. Then and only then will we find moral stamina for the battles which lie ahead.

If and when we have submitted our ordinary lives to God, the next step is for us to *resist*.

254

Resist the Devil and He Will Flee

The Greek word for "resist" in James 4:7 is ἀνθίστημι. It means *to set oneself against; to oppose.*[194] This word calls for an active, not passive, resistance.

Merriam Webster defines the English verb "resist" in this way:

1. to exert force in opposition;
2. to exert oneself so as to counteract or defeat;
3. to withstand the force or effect of[195]

The meaning of the Greek word in James 4 undoubtedly includes that third "standing firm" aspect of resistance, but it especially emphasizes the first two aspects. Resistance requires a deliberate step, a deliberate action.

Christians are never supposed to just stand by silently and watch the devil do his work. We are to stand up and take bold, decisive action *against him.* We have to counteract his efforts and work hard to expose his lies, deceptions, and schemes. We have to exert ourselves—expend real energy—*in the opposition against evil.*

God has dropped an urgent and critical mission in our laps today. The lights in this nation are growing dimmer and dimmer with every day that passes. *It's time to resist.*

Resistance means taking action against evil with a clear intent to win. Resisting the devil means that when he arrives, he finds us running out to meet him with slingshot and stone in hand. [196]

And then, God says,

He will flee from you!

There is no power greater than the power of our God! When God's people turn back to His ordinary design for their lives; and when they take decisive action to oppose evil, *the devil must flee.*

Evil doesn't stand a chance.

Overcoming the Malady of Christian Paralysis

The devil is indeed having his day in the United States of America. He is destroying our nation with lies. He is tearing America to shreds with false promises. He is catching many of us unaware in a great wide web of delusions.

And so many Christians are frozen! So many of us are just sitting on the sidelines watching. Why? Why are we just allowing the government to take away our freedom? Why are we so unable to defend our core beliefs?

Both Solzhenitsyn and Bonhoeffer identify in their writings a hauntingly familiar, debilitating, and deadly passivity that was prevalent among supposed God-fearing people in both pre-Soviet Russia and pre-Nazi Germany. Far too many people in both of those nations were caught unprepared *to resist*; and as a result, they were swept away by the lies.

Both Bonhoeffer and Solzhenitsyn believed that this tragic failure of good people to *resist evil* when evil showed up on their doorstep was in no small part to blame for the collapse of biblically valid, if imperfect, forms of government in those two countries.

The ordinary actions of believers carry far more weight and influence than we can begin to comprehend. New Testament scholar Dr. Craig Keener writes,

> The church, no matter how powerless in a given society, is a guardian of its culture. Just as the presence of the righteous in Sodom was the only factor that could have restrained judgment (Gen. 18:20-32), the fate of a culture may depend ultimately on the behavior of the believers in that culture.[197]

What we, God's people, do or do not do today in this critical moment of America's history *matters*. All of heaven's hosts and all future generations are waiting breathlessly to see how God's people are going to react to the evil of tyranny threatening us today.

What was at the root of the costly passivity among the God-fearing in Germany and Russia last century? It's important to know, so we can dig it out of ourselves!

Solzhenitsyn is pointed in his criticism of a "Christianity" that lies dormant and passive in the face of evil. In *The Red Wheel*, he goes to poetic lengths to describe the prevailing spiritual attitude of Russian "Christians" in the early 20th century. At that time in Russia, there were a plethora of truths from which the spiritually-inclined could choose, but Leo Tolstoy was an especially popular spiritual hero in Russia and it was fashionable to follow his views.

Tolstoy was an apostate. He had left the traditional Christian faith and created his own version of "Christianity" based purely on his understanding of the Sermon on the Mount. He rejected the Old Testament and all the parts of the New Testament he didn't think belonged there, and his new beliefs led him and his followers straight to pacifism. He believed military service was wrong and went further than that. He believed all violence, even that exerted by the government *to protect its people*, was wrong; and because of that belief, he discouraged his followers away from taking part in anything that was remotely connected with politics or government.[198]

Tolstoy preached a smooth message of love, peace, and nonresistance: Don't judge anyone else's beliefs. Don't rock that boat. If we just love everyone hard enough and educate them more, everything will change for the better. Pursue "love" and pursue deep spirituality, but don't ever get involved in anything that has anything to do with this world. Above all, don't touch government or civic affairs.[199]

Daniel Mahoney, a contributing writer for *First Things*, writes, on Solzhenitsyn,

> Why, then, is Solzhenitsyn so hard on the pacifistic distortion of Christianity? Because evil is real, rooted in fallen human nature, and must be resisted if the things of the soul are to be preserved. The state is a powerful instrument for keeping evil at bay and for safeguarding the foundations of civilized order. One must resist the facile negation of the common good, which is so typical of Tolstoy. The spirit of pacifism also dulls one to the malign efforts of those revolutionary nihilists such as the Bolsheviks, committed as they were to the destruction of Christian civilization. Against Tolstoy, Solzhenitsyn urges what he once called "the active struggle against evil," which entails the maintenance of an imperfect order against ideological demons who are animated only by the spirit of pure revolutionary negation.[200]

Tolstoy's version of love wasn't the brand of love we see exemplified in Jesus Christ when He put himself in harm's way, laid His own life down, suffered, and died to overcome evil and save His people from the grip of sin. All Tolstoy did was stand back and watch.

Bonhoeffer noticed similar passive and detached attitudes in pre-Nazi Germany. Biographer Eric Metaxas writes, "He began to see that the overemphasis on the cerebral and intellectual side of theological training had produced pastors who didn't know how to live as Christians."[201]

In Germany, Christianity had become a mere intellectual exercise. Bonhoeffer mourned the fact that Christianity was no longer understood as the Bible teaches it to be: an all-encompassing, life-consuming, illusion-shattering reality and mission we are called to live out with our bodies *here on earth* for the benefit of the Kingdom to come.

"Who stands fast?" he asked. "Only the man whose final standard is not his reason, his principles, his conscience, his freedom, or his virtue, but who is ready to sacrifice all this when he is called to obedient and responsible action in faith and exclusive allegiance to God—the responsible man who makes his whole life an answer to the call of God."[202]

Metaxas goes on to explain,

He [Bonhoeffer] had theologically redefined the Christian life as something active, not reactive. It had nothing to do with avoiding sin or with merely talking or teaching or believing theological notions or principles or rules or tenets. It had everything to do with living one's whole life in obedience to God's call through action. It did not merely require a mind, but a body too. It was God's call to be fully human, to live as human beings obedient to the one who had made us, which was the fulfillment of our destiny. "Mere waiting and looking on is not Christian behavior. The Christian is called to sympathy and to action, not in the first place by his own sufferings, but by the sufferings of his brethren, for whose sake Christ suffered."[203]

Where Have We Gone Wrong?

Let's take an honest look around us. What has happened to God-fearing America?

Are we not listening to peace, love, and non-resistance teachers who sound just like Tolstoy? It is painfully unfashionable today to be considered patriotic, and it is shameful for good spiritual Christians to talk about politics. Right in step with the world, many of us are backing away from supporting any kind of violence, even necessary violence enacted by government and law enforcement to protect human life and God-given, basic human rights.

Have we not splintered apart the spiritual aspects of our lives from the physical, *which God has joined together?* In the Christian world today, "ministry" is often seen as all-important while "ordinary living" holds no real value. This distortion of truth is keeping us from putting our faith into action in the real world. It is keeping us from presenting every moment, every breath, and every activity of our lives to the Lord as a holy and living sacrifice.

Does not the evangelical world today also sound like the intellectually-bloated church of pre-Nazi Germany? Much of "Christianity" in America has become dangerously unhinged from Eternal Truth. Our theological understanding has reached such scholarly heights that we believe we have the right to pick and choose what parts of the Bible we prefer. How we delude ourselves!

Some of us are just depressed and discouraged. Our faith is waning. We believe it's too late for our words and actions to do any good.

Dear friends, it's time to turn back to God's ordinary. It's time to re-integrate spiritual knowledge and Eternal Truth with ordinary, physical life in the real, physical world. It's time to strengthen our faith. *And it's time to turn our faith into action.*

A Biblical View of God and Government

In his novel *August 1914 (The Red Wheel Part One)* Solzhenitsyn wrote, "The laws for constructing the best social order must be inherent in the structure of the world as a whole. In the design behind the universe is man's destiny."[204]

Just as Truth tells me how to live my ordinary life in my own home and community, Truth also tells the governments of this earth how they are meant to govern. God says, speaking of His Eternal wisdom and Truth, "By me kings reign, and rulers decree justice. By me princes rule, and nobles, all who judge rightly." Proverbs 8:15, 16

God's Word has laid out a basic design every legitimate government is supposed to follow. The institution of the state was created by God to protect citizens from violence. To protect the human rights which He gave them. It exists to enforce the law and uphold true justice so that ordinary people can freely and safely go about living their ordinary lives according to God's plan.

> "For the Lord's sake, submit to all human authority—whether the king as head of state, or the officials he has appointed. For the king has sent them *to punish those who do wrong and to honor those who do right*." I Peter 2:13, 14 (italics added)

> "I urge you, first of all, to pray for all people. Ask God to help them; intercede on their behalf, and give thanks for them. Pray this way for kings and all who are in authority *so that we can live peaceful and quiet lives marked by godliness and dignity*." I Timothy 2:1, 2 (italics added)

The United States is facing a dire emergency today not only because ordinary people are ditching God's ordinary in their personal lives, but because this rebellion has snowballed to such an extent that our government is in grave and immediate danger of unhinging from God's design as well; for, "When there is moral rot within a nation, its government topples easily..." Proverbs 28:2

This spells disaster for America. It means God's design for the restriction of violence, oppression, and injustice on this sinful earth is about to be thrown out, leaving nothing standing between U.S. citizens and tyranny.

Every Christian's Responsibility

What is an ordinary God-fearing person supposed to do in this situation? We have to remember today that we are not just part of a family, and a church, and a community. *We are part of a nation, too.*

When the state is functioning at least generally according to God's design, Christians are clearly called to submit to the laws of the government. What happens, though, when a government begins straying from its God-given design...or when its legitimacy is at risk of dissolution? At that time what is the proper response of the Christian and of the church? Are we to sit by silently and watch what appears to be inevitable? Or are we supposed to take action to try and stop it? What is the right thing to do?

Our generation in America has never really had to wrestle with these questions on a personal level, but today we must.

Last century, as Germany's Rule of Law protecting individual rights was being traded away for madness and tyranny, church leader Dietrich Bonhoeffer studied this question himself extensively. Eric Metaxas writes, summarizing Bonhoeffer's conclusion,

> Governments are established by God for the preservation of order. "Without a doubt, the Church of the Reformation has no right to address the state directly in its specifically political actions."

> Then he moved on to clarify that the church does, nonetheless, play a vital role for the state. What is that role? The church must "continually ask the state whether its action can be justified as legitimate action of the state, i.e., as action which leads to law and order, and not to lawlessness and disorder." In other words, it is the church's role to help the state be the state. If the state is not creating an atmosphere of law

and order, as Scriptures says it must, then it is the job of the church to draw attention to this failing. And if on the other hand, the state is creating an atmosphere of "excessive law and order," it is the church's job to draw attention to that too.

If the state is creating "excessive law and order," then "the state develops its power to such an extent that it deprives Christian preaching and Christian faith...of their rights." Bonhoeffer called this a "grotesque situation." "The church," he said, "must reject this encroachment of the order of the state precisely because of its better knowledge of the state and of the limitations of its action. The state which endangers the Christian proclamation negates itself."[205]

There is a lot of wisdom in these words. Sometimes we forget that as God's people we are not only witnesses of the mystery of God's "special grace," which is the Gospel of salvation by grace through faith in Jesus Christ; we are also witnesses of the mystery of God's "common grace"—which includes His temporary plan for restraining evil on earth: government by a just rule of law.

So the church has a very important role when it comes to government affairs. We are to *speak up* when the government begins straying from its God-given job. We are to *speak up* and *act against* any such movement and do our best to help the government stay aligned with its God-intended design.

If the state starts to overstep its God-given boundaries as state and begins to give orders that restrict religious freedom or "ordinary life" according to God's design, the church has a responsibility to *resist this overstepping*.

When the government (or any other arm of tyranny) begins telling us to stop living *God's ordinary*, we are released from our orders to submit and must instead *resist*.

Called to Resist

Do you know that in the 1700s many if not most of the leaders of the Minute-Men in the Revolutionary War were pastors? From the pulpit, these pastors taught their congregations about the real-life evils of tyranny and through the power of God drilled a conviction into their hearts that they each had a God-given responsibility as human beings living with flesh and bones in a sinful world *to resist it!*

These courageous pastors spoke this powerful message from the pulpit, then they took their men outside on the grass and drilled them with muskets for battle. When evil tyranny arrived on their doorstep dressed in red coats, it didn't stand a chance because it found men of God who were poised and ready with a rock-solid moral resolve to defeat it.

Ordinary Americans laid down their safety, their comfort, and their lives out a firm conviction that to support a God-honoring, theologically-legitimate form of government was part of their calling as flesh and blood Christians who live real lives in a physical world infested with real, deadly evil. To fight against the oppression of evil tyranny was a natural extension of their faith in God and their commitment to Jesus Christ, and *every single one of us has reaped the blessings and benefits of their dedicated resolve!*

In an article for Christian Heritage Ministries, Dr. Catherine Millard writes, "Pulpit preaching in the Protestant churches of America provided the moral force which won her independence."[206] Thank God for courageous pastors! *Pastors, we need you again today!*

The time has come for the Church to take a stand. We have it on the authority of God's Word that whenever and wherever people are willing to both submit to God and to actively resist evil, *the devil will flee.*

264

History is not completely out of our hands. God is sovereign over all, but His people play a vital role in determining which way the river of history will flow. If we, the interpreters and keepers of the mystery of God's design, stop leading and pointing the way—or worse, let go of our guiding rope altogether!—how does the river stand a chance of finding which way it should go?

We human beings discover our destiny *when we surrender our lives to Jesus Christ and stick unswervingly to the pathway of His design.*

Where Resistance Is Needed

Where is the devil at work in America right now? Where do we need to resist?

He is not coming at us with guns and ammunition at the moment; he is attacking us with delusions and lies.

- The lie that the local church is nonessential in times of crisis.

- The lie that sin resides in collectives and originates in systems rather than residing and originating in individual human hearts.

- The lie that fighting for justice equals voting for destructive socialist policies.

- The lie that the road to true freedom means mob rule, collective mass judgments, and trashing a higher rule of law.

- The lie that overbearing monopolies are the result of capitalism and not the result of socialist interference in the free market via subsidies.

- The lie that equality means we should all be the same and that everyone should own an equal amount of wealth.

- The lie that Christianity and Marxism are basically the same.

- The lie that humans are subject to nature, and that we must make sacrifices to appease mother earth.

- The lie that we can control disease and death!

- The lie that to be truly liberated, moms have to choose a career over raising their own children.

- The lie that our sex lives and the way we handle our money are only about *us* and don't affect anyone else.

- The lie that abortion is anything other than evil genocide.

- The lie that Christians are supposed to keep people happy and never offend anyone.

- The lie that Christianity is supposed to stay within the walls of the church and never interact with the rest of real life, and that the church can't ever address anything remotely connected with politics.

- The lie that says men should act like women and women should act like men.

- The lie that it is shameful to love one's own culture or to be patriotic or to be active, involved citizens of a state.

- The lie that the concept of a constitutional republic is meaningless and that it doesn't matter if our government folds or not.

- The lie that there's nothing God's people can do in the day of evil except surrender to it.

There is only one weapon strong enough to overcome the Lie: *Truth*.

Men and women of America, if God has opened up your eyes to the evil this country is facing, *join the resistance today*. Whatever your gift, whatever your talent, whatever your audience, whatever your platform...large or small...use it. Take up the sword of Truth and march into battle with it. Don't bow down to oppression. Ask God to show you how you can *push back* against it.

And I hope and pray and beg God that this day will never come, but if the day does come when we need to resist tyranny with force and take up arms to protect legitimate human rights; then our Christian duty as citizens in a physical world that faces physical threats of real violence and tangible evil is for us to *resist evil* in this way as well.

Resisting evil may look impossible and dangerous to us today; but we only need to look at Communist China, Soviet Russia, Nazi Germany, and all other previous socialist experiments in misery and death to realize that the far more dangerous option is for us to remain passive. The day has come for us to join what Solzhenitsyn called the "active struggle against evil."

> Therefore, since we are surrounded by such a great cloud of witnesses, let us throw off everything that hinders and the sin that so easily entangles. And let us run with perseverance the race marked out for us, fixing our eyes on Jesus, the pioneer and perfecter of faith. For the joy set before Him he endured the cross, scorning its shame, and sat down at the right hand of the throne of God. Consider him who endured such opposition from sinners, so that you will not grow weary and lose heart. In your struggle against sin, you have not yet resisted to the point of shedding your blood. Hebrews 12:1-4

What if, when the Bible says, "If you confess with your mouth and believe in your heart then you will be saved," "confessing with our mouths" is more than just muttering some magic words under our breath at the altar or campfire?

What if confessing with our mouths (or "openly declaring," as the NLT says) means having the kind of faith—the kind of *belief*—that compels us to stand up in front a culture that hates us; a culture screaming at us that we're supremacists, homophobes, climate change deniers, fascists, bigots, and enemies of justice to say with conviction,

I still believe in the eternal and unchanging Truth of Almighty God!

I still believe that true freedom, justice, and equality are found only when we surrender to Him!

God is questioning us today.

Who among us is willing?

"As surely as I live, says the Sovereign Lord, I take no pleasure in the death of wicked people. I only want them to turn from their wicked ways so they can live. Turn! Turn from your wickedness, O people of Israel! Why should you die?"

—Ezekiel 33:11

19

A FINAL MESSAGE FOR MY COUNTRY

TURN AROUND

From just behind us—if we will stop;
stop just for a moment to listen—
from right behind us comes a voice.
The voice is still and small. Barely a whisper.
But it is crystal clear;
    and piercing in its intensity.
Turn!
The voice calls out to us, filled with longing.
It pleads. It commands.
It invites!
Turn around.
Get rid of your foreign gods.
Return your heart to Me.

Today we have a choice.

Our choice is this:

It's **Him**.

Him!

Him!

Him,

or our stubborn pride.

If we will obey His voice; if we will listen to Him now…

If we will just *turn around*…

We will come face to face

with a Man.

You know who He is.

His eyes are kindled;

they are glowing, flickering, sparking embers…

of great love.

Love!

Love.

Go ahead! Look into them for yourself!

Come unto Me, He says,

Enter the gate!

Listen!

I will give you rest.

Be still…

for I am God.

His voice grows louder and louder.

It rushes through our hearts like the movement of many waters.

I have broken the curse!

I hung on a tree.

His Truth peals out like thunder.

It is finished.

His arms are open. He is waiting for you.

You.

One step.

One whispered prayer.

One tiny glance of faith into His eyes of love.

That's all it takes, dear friend.

Do not be afraid.

Repent and believe.

He is a Man, and He is the King.

Lightning flashes around His throne.

His throne! It's surrounded by an emerald glow...like a rainbow.

He is not like us.

He is greater than us.

He is God,

The One True God,

The Creator of all things.

Come!

I AM the Source.

Truth, love, justice, peace!

I AM the King.

Fall down on your knees!
I AM the Lord.
Shining brighter than the sun!
In Me, you may have peace,
for I AM…
Life.

♽

We aren't able to lift the burdens of suffering humanity;
We can't cancel the power of death.
But *He* breaks the chains of captives!
He sets the prisoners free!
Can't you see?!
He stood up, left the riches of His throne, and became dirt poor...
to join *our great struggle* for freedom.
He won what we could not win,
and offers it now to us *for free.*

♽

The problem with the earth is *us,* my friend.
It's not *them.*
The problem is you and the problem is me.
We have sinned.
We have raised our fists to His face!
We have rebelled.

But He can wash us clean.

He wants to set us free.

Repent and believe.

∽○∽

I test the heart, He says.

I am the God Who Sees...

how you *crave* fulfillment, *long* for justice, *desire* freedom, *dream* of equality, *clutch* at safety,

thirst for love.

Drink!

He says.

Drink deeply!

Anyone who is thirsty may come and drink,

Drink freely from the Wellspring of Life.

All these things...and so much more...can be ours...

They just don't come through the power of what humans can do!

They're not discovered in the redistribution of wealth.

They're not won through democracy.

They're not reached by environmental consciousness.

They're not achieved by destroying the economy.

They're not found in new heights of technology.

They're not waiting to be discovered deep inside ourselves.

It is for freedom that I have set you free!

∞o∞

This Man…His name is **Jesus**.

He gently comforts the oppressed woman and clothes her with dignity.

He comes alongside the weary worker and infuses his labor with purpose.

He whispers to all the children who rest, snuggled safely in His arms...

(for He knows our world is scary, He sees the monsters, too)

I am like a lion!

And at My roar all the earth trembles.

But I will be a refuge for My people,

A safe place for them to hide.

To all you who are mistreated, lonely, overlooked, persecuted, or eyed with prejudice:

He sees you.

He knows your name.

He loves you.

He cares.

He has collected your tears in His bottle. He has recorded each one in His book.

Vengeance is Mine and I will repay, says the Lord.

He is familiar, too, with the burdens of the poor!

"Therefore do not worry, saying, 'What shall we eat?' or 'What shall we drink?' or 'What shall we wear?'...Seek first the kingdom of God and His righteousness, and all these things shall be added to you." Matthew 6:31, 33

His voice rings out to the courageous, the warriors, the brave!

Follow Me;

I will train your hands for war

so your arms can bend a bow of bronze.

> "For we are not fighting against flesh-and-blood
> enemies, but against evil rulers and authorities of
> the unseen world, against mighty powers in this dark
> world, and against evil spirits in the heavenly places."
> Psalm 18:34

And to all the inhabitants of the earth:

He understands there's something terribly wrong with our earthly home.

It is wearing out.

It is quaking and fuming and smoking with His rage!

It is exploding with His awful wrath.

His anger is fierce against us and our sin.

It's because of the curse! It's because of our sin! It's because of our deadly pride!

We can't slow the earth's violent end with regulations; we can't stop it with all the money and rituals in the world.

But we don't have to be afraid!

Hurry! Before it's too late!

He forgives!

He rescues!

He saves.

Behold, I am making all things...

new.

✣

To the nations this is His eternal vow:

If you obey My voice, your towns and your fields will be blessed. Your children and your crops will be blessed. The offspring of your herds and flocks will be blessed. Your fruit baskets and breadboards will be blessed. Wherever you go and whatever you do, you will be blessed.

If you do not obey My voice, your towns and your fields will be cursed. Your fruit baskets and breadboards will be cursed. Your children and your crops will be cursed. The offspring of your herds and flocks will be cursed. Wherever you go and whatever you do, you will be cursed. Deuteronomy 28

Which will we choose?

Come to Me!

He is waiting for us.

Come.

Don't turn Him away.

Come.

"If you openly declare that Jesus is Lord and believe in your heart that God raised Him from the dead, you will be saved." Romans 10:9

AFTERWORD

There was a particular time early on in my research for this book when I felt I was getting lost in the darkness. Devastated by all the harsh realities swirling around me, I began to sink emotionally under their weight. During this time I was reading Solzhenitsyn's epic work *The Gulag Archipelago*.[207]

It was the darkest period of my research.

The Gulag Archipelago is a difficult read, to say the least. It is the three-volume, factual account of the enslavement, torture, and death of tens of millions of citizens who were sent to suffer and die in Soviet Russia's labor/reeducation camps in frigid Siberia.

Starvation. Frozen, emaciated bodies. Rampant disease. Cruel, inhumane conditions.

All this emerged out of an initial noble-sounding rallying cry for "peace, land, and bread."[208]

The kind of darkness described in this book is incomprehensible. It is ghastly and sickening.

Yet something spurred me on through the pages; I had to keep reading.

On and on I waded through the horrors.

I had to face them. I had to grapple with the real depths of evil and suffering that are possible on this earth. All this happened through and to human beings just like me. Just like you. Just like *us*.

As I continued through the book I felt like I was also searching for something else; waiting for something, I didn't know what. I just kept reading.

Eventually, I found it. I found what I had been so desperate to find.

Surprisingly, *The Gulag Archipelago* does not leave its readers completely buried and suffocating in an inescapable pit of despair as one might expect. Volume Two, which recounts in detail some of the greatest suffering human beings have experienced in the history of this earth, ends, shockingly—on a clear, high note.

Even though many people just shriveled up and were absolutely corrupted inside the evil walls of the Soviet slave labor camps…although so many sank in the pit of hell that was that place never to rise again; many others, Solzhenitsyn shares with conviction, *ascended*.[209]

Whether by life or by death, they *rose above the clutches of the pit*.

They defeated the darkness.

They won!

They weren't pummeled, pushed down, and drowned by the floodwaters of evil. No! The great flood-tide only lifted them up higher…and higher…and higher…until they stood victorious on top of its waves.

They accomplished this incredible feat by taking to heart the deep lessons that came from suffering and *by holding onto Truth, even inside the darkness, and never letting go*.

Solzhenitsyn tells of Christians who were always anomalies inside the camp; who remained self-confident and steadfast to the end and seemed to carry everywhere they went some invisible Light wholly foreign to the rest of the prisoners.[210]

It was in the Gulag that Solzhenitsyn himself, forced by suffering to acknowledge the evil residing in his own heart, rediscovered the faith in God he had previously renounced… *and ascended to the top of the waves*.

During his prison camp experience, Solzhenitsyn came face to face with visible, tangible evil; but he also encountered something else. *Someone else.* There was a moment when he came to the stunning realization that although he—along with nearly everyone else in his country—had walked away from God, *God had never walked away from him.*

God was calling out to him!

God still loved Russia, and He still loved the communist rebel Aleksandr Solzhenitsyn. In exile, lying near death in a cancer ward, Solzhenitsyn discovered that God had been right there all along—waiting for him with open arms and a heart full of forgiveness and love.

After a miraculous recovery, he composed a poem in the recovery room and stored it away in his mind. The poem ended with these words:

> *And now with measuring cup returned to me,*
> *Scooping up the living water,*
> *God of the Universe! I believe again!*
> *Though I renounced You, You were with me!* [211]

It turns out that God's greatest acts of judgment upon this earth are simultaneously His greatest acts of mercy. They are His last-ditch attempts to shake us human beings awake from our slumber of death so that we might find Life…*before it's too late.*

God's invitation remains open today for America to *turn around*; but even if America refuses—even if this nation has to endure the *very worst*—we can rest assured that the *very worst* can't defeat anyone protected by the blood of Jesus Christ.

For us, the *very worst* can only result in greater opportunities to stand witness to God's Truth and love and faithfulness. The *very worst* can only lead to deeper faith and more glory to God. The *very worst* can only catapult us to victory!

O death, where is your victory? O death, where is your sting?

There remains on this earth a Beauty that cannot be crushed by the vilest, blackest schemes of darkness. There exists a Hope that the fullest weight of united human rebellion and wickedness cannot and will not ever stamp out. It is the reality of one holy, loving, pure, and Almighty God.

Take comfort, dear world. Be filled with joy!

There is darkness, yes.

But there is a Light shining in the darkness, and the darkness cannot overcome it.

Let your light shine!

ACKNOWLEDGMENTS

I would like to thank, first of all, my parents; for passing down to me the extraordinary gift of *ordinary living*. My dad's gentle, calloused, oil-stained hands; the flour-dusted rolling pin in my mom's; and all the miles on all those cars from driving us back and forth to church all those years—they tell the story. Mom and dad, *thank you*.

Courtney, you have always made ordinary so much fun! You never fail to have just the pep talk I need ready and waiting in your pocket. You are a gift and I love you!

Grammy, Mimi, Papa, and all of my wonderful Vermont family...also my church family from EDBC back in the day... you have all given me the priceless gift of your beautiful ordinary, too. I am grateful and I love you all. "To whom much is given, much will be required." *I have been given so very much!*

Amanda, thank you for "holding up my hands" (Ex. 17:12) on Thursdays these past months, and for allowing me to hold up yours! Laurie, Katy, & Bethany, thank you too for praying me through this entire battle and all its ups and downs. God knows I couldn't make it through this life without you three. Megan, kindred spirit and treasured friend, thank you for reaching out again at just the right time. Judy, thank you for your patient listening ear as Josh and I initially struggled so hard to hear the message God wanted to give us through *ordinary!* What a journey.

And Katy, *thank you*. Your wisdom, keen editor's eye, and cheering have meant so very much. You helped make this book what it is.

Aleksandr Solzhenitsyn and Dietrich Bonhoeffer, I have come to believe that your legacies are a direct gift from God to our generation so we would not be left without wise counsel in our hour of trial. I, for one, am listening. Someday I will thank you myself in heaven for the priceless treasures you left us.

My brothers and sisters in China…thank you too for the gift of your friendship and culture, and for giving us Americans an example of what it means to *keep on living ordinary* even in the face of darkness. My family prays every day for a free China!

Mom and Dad P, thank you so much for Josh, for your friendship, for moving close, for Friday nights off, and for encouraging me to keep writing! Your suggestions for revisions were such a tremendous help.

K&V, thank you for praying with such confidence and faith that this book would get done "in time," (sometimes it looks like He's running late but He always arrives on time!), and for making sure I included John 3:16. It's in here! The two of you are my heart's delight; *you are my gift and my reward.*

Josh—the love of my life and my partner in all things ordinary, we arrived here together. Thank you for seeing, even before I did, that there was something I needed to say. Your strength and wisdom give me courage. This book wouldn't be possible without you; you make all my dreams come true. Thank you. *I love you so much.*

And Jesus, My precious Jesus. You are my God and my King forever; my only Savior and my dearest Friend. Your perfect love is stronger than fear! I am loved and I am free! *All blessing and honor and glory and power are Yours…both now and forever.* My cup overflows. Thank You for choosing an ordinary woman like me.

God of mercy, sweet Love of mine,
I have surrendered to Your design.
May this offering spread across the skies,
These hallelujahs be multiplied!

—"Multiplied"[212]

NOTES

1 *China: A Century of Revolution*. Dir. Sue Williams. 1997. DVD. This three-part series can (at least for now) be watched for free in its entirety on *YouTube*.

2 Ibid.

3 Ollman, Bertell. "A Model of Activist Research: How to Study Class Consciousness...and Why We Should." n.d. *nyu.edu*. 15 August 2020.

4 Somin, Ilya. "Remembering the Biggest Mass Murder in the History of the World." 3 August 2016. *washingtonpost.com*. 22 July 2020.

5 Ollman, Bertell. "Marx's Vision of Communism." n.d. *nyu.edu*. 26 April 2020.

6 Merriam-Webster. *merriam-webster.com*. n.d. 11 April 2019.

7 Fox News. "Obama to Business Owners: 'You Didn't Build That'." 16 July 2012. *foxnews.com*. 28 February 2020.

8 Brooks, Mick. "An Introduction to Marx's Labour Theory of Value." 12 July 2005. *marxist.com*. 24 February 2020.

9 Horwitz, Steven. "We're Still Haunted by the Labor Theory of Value." 12 November 2015. *fee.org.* 27 February 2020.

10 Isaiah 64:6, Matthew 10:31, Ephesians 1:4.

11 Horwitz, Steven. "We're Still Haunted by the Labor Theory of Value." 12 November 2015. *Foundation for Economic Education* . 27 February 2020.

12 DiLorenzo, Thomas. *The Problem with Socialism*. Washington, DC: Regnery Publishing, 2016. 116.

13 Merriam-Webster. *merriam-webster.com*. n.d. 11 April 2019.

14 Democracy Now. "Vermont's Bernie Sanders Becomes First Socialist Elected to U.S. Senate." 8 November 2006. *democracynow.org.* 16 August 2019.

15 Polybius. (2014). The Complete Histories of Polybius. (W.R. Paton, Translator) Digireads.com Publishing. 522, 523.

16 Democratic Socialists of America. "What is Democratic Socialism?" 15 July 2008. *dsa.org.* 23 August 2019.

17 Hayek, F. A. *The Road to Serfdom.* Routledge: The University of Chicago Press, 2007. 138.

18 Solzhenitsyn, Alexander. *Warning to the West.* New York: Farrar, Straus and Giroux, 1976. 141, 142.

19 Shafarevich, Igor. *The Socialist Phenomenon.* The United States of America: Gideon House Books, 2019. 18, 19.

20 Ibid. 18.

21 Ibid. 224, 225.

22 Ibid. 292.

23 Merriam-Webster. *merriam-webster.com.* n.d. 11 April 2019.

24 Solzhenitsyn, Alexander. *Warning to the West.* New York: Farrar, Straus and Giroux, 1976. 129, 130.

25 Bezmenov, Yuri. "Soviet Subversion of the Free World Press (Complete Interview)." *YouTube,* uploaded by elixirgroove, 17 February 2017, https://www.youtube.com/watch?v=LnRNFRBVv5Q.

26 Bezmenov, Yuri. "Yuri Bezmenov (Tomas Shuman)—Ideological Subversion." *YouTube,* uploaded by Marlsa, 25 August 2018, https://www.youtube.com/watch?v=KLdDmeyMJls.

27 Sun, Tzu. *The Art of War.* Black & White Classics, 2014.

28 Bezmenov, Yuri. "Yuri Bezmenov (Tomas Shuman)—Ideological Subversion." *YouTube,* uploaded by Marlsa, 25 August 2018, https://www.youtube.com/watch?v=KLdDmeyMJls.

29 Ibid.

30 Ibid.

31 Hayek, F. A. *The Road to Serfdom*. Routledge: The University of Chicago Press, 2007. 89.

32 I found similar lists in several places, including *libertyzone.com* and *laissez-fairerepublic.com*. Props to whomever first assembled these comparisons.

33 Feagin, Joe R. *Systemic Racism: A Theory of Oppression*. New York: Routledge, 2006. 42.

34 Hayek, F. A. *The Road to Serfdom*. Routledge: The University of Chicago Press, 2007. 50.

35 Shafarevich, Igor. *The Socialist Phenomenon*. The United States of America: Gideon House Books, 2019. 11.

36 Cooper, Ryan. "America's Constitution is terrible. Let's throw it out and start over." 2018 26 January. *theweek.com*. 17 December 2019.

37 Hayek, F. A. *The Road to Serfdom*. Routledge: The University of Chicago Press, 2007. 116, 119.

38 DiLorenzo, Thomas. *The Problem with Socialism*. Washington, DC: Regnery Publishing, 2016. 56-65, 130.

39 Hayek, F. A. *The Road to Serfdom*. Routledge: The University of Chicago Press, 2007. 58, 59.

40 Shepherd, Robin. "So, how many did Communism kill?" 5 October 2013. *thecommentator.com*. 16 June 2020.

41 Courtois, Werth, Panne, Paczkowski, Bartosek, Margolin. *The Black Book of Communism: Crimes, Terror, Repression*. The United States of America: Harvard University Press, 1999.

42 Solzhenitsyn, Alexander. *Warning to the West*. New York: Farrar, Straus and Giroux, 1976. 129.

43 Barua, Bacchus, Nadeem Esmail and Taylor Jackson. "The Effect of Wait Times on Mortality in Canada." Mat 2014. *fraserinstitute.org*. 24 April 2020.

44 American-Israeli Cooperative Enterprise (AICE). "The "Final Solution": Estimated Number of Jews Killed." n.d. *Jewish Virtual Library.* 24 April 2020.

45 Sanger, Margaret. *The Pivot of Civilization.* Read Books, 2016. 6.

46 Ibid. 106, 111.

47 Ludwig, Hayden. "Margaret Sanger: Sterilization." 19 May 2020. *capitalresearch.org.* 22 June 2020.

48 Sanger, Margaret. "What Every Girl Should Know: Sexual Impulses Part II." 1912 December 29. *nyu.edu.* 22 June 2020.

49 Sanger, Margaret. *The Pivot of Civilization.* Read Books, 2016. 31, 131, 66.

50 Ibid. 193.

51 Caruba, Lauren. "More black babies are aborted in NYC than born." 25 November 2015. *politifact.com.* 27 April 2020.

52 Merriam-Webster. *learnersdictionary.com.* n.d. 25 January 2020.

53 Ollman, Bertell. "Alienation: Marx's Conception of Man in Capitalist Society Part III, The Theory of Alienation." n.d. *nyu. edu.* 28 April 2020.

54 Ibid.

55 Van Susteren, Dirk; Davis, Neil. "Sanders Spurns Tradition to Change People's Heads." *The Burlington Free Press,* 3 October 1976.

56 Cole, Nicki Lisa. "Definition of Base and Superstructure." 24 January 2020. *thoughtco.com.* 8 August 2020.

57 Marx, Karl. "marxists.org." 1845. *Theses On Feuerbach.* 17 June 2020.

58 Marx, Karl. "Critique of the Gotha Programme, Part IV." 1875. *marxists.org.* 7 August 2020.

59 Marx, Karl. "Manifesto of the Communist Party." 1847. *marxists.org.* 7 August 2020. II.

60 D'Amato, Paul. "Marx vs. the Myth of Human Nature." 4 November 2011. *socialistworker.org.* 17 June 2020.

61 Shafarevich, Igor. *The Socialist Phenomenon.* The United States of America: Gideon House Books, 2019. 317.

62 Ibid.

63 Solzhenitsyn, Aleksandr. *August 1914: A Novel (The Red Wheel I).* New York: Farrar, Straus and Giroux; Reprint Edition, 2014. Loc. 4245, 4546, 4572.

64 Solzhenitsyn, Aleksandr. *Warning to the West.* New York: Farrar, Straus and Giroux, 1976. 53.

65 Ibid. 72, 73.

66 Ibid. 53, 82.

67 Ollman, Bertell. "Alienation: Marx's Conception of Man in Capitalist Society Part III, The Theory of Alienation." n.d. *nyu. edu.* 28 April 2020.

68 Ollman, Bertell. "A Bird's Eye View of Socialism." n.d. *nyu.edu.* 28 April 2020.

69 Schwartz, Joseph and Jason Schulman. "Toward Freedom: Democratic Socialist Theory and Practice." 12 December 2012. *dsausa.org.* 28 April 2020.

70 Democratic Socialists of America. "Resistance Rising: Socialist Strategy in the Age of Political Revolution." 25 June 2016. *dsausa.org.* 28 April 2020.

71 DiLorenzo, Thomas. *The Problem with Socialism.* Washington, DC: Regnery Publishing, 2016. 23-32.

72 Solzhenitsyn, Aleksandr. "Godlessness: the First Step to the Gulag." *Templeton Prize Lecture.* London, 10 May 1983. 24 April 2020.

73 Shafarevich, Igor. *The Socialist Phenomenon.* The United States of America: Gideon House Books, 2019. 264, 265.

74 Bezmenov, Yuri. "Yuri Bezmenov (Tomas Shuman)— Ideological Subversion." *YouTube*, uploaded by

Marlsa, 25 August 2018, https://www.youtube.com/watch?v=KLdDmeyMJls.

75 Ibid.

76 Metaxas, Eric. *Bonhoeffer Pastor, Martyr, Prophet, Spy*. Nashville: Thomas Nelson, 2010. 125.

77 Solzhenitsyn, Aleksandr. *The Gulag Archipelago One*. Harper & Row; 1st edition, 1973, 1974. 202.

78 John 15:13; Ephesians 5, 6; Genesis 2:18; Titus 2:4, 5; Proverbs 1:8; Proverbs 13:24; Proverbs 22:6; Deuteronomy 11:19; I Timothy 5:4, 8.

79 I John 4:8.

80 Willard, Dallas. *Living in Christ's Presence*. Downer's Grove: InterVarsity Press, 2014. 98-99.

81 Genesis 2:23, 24; Hebrews 13:4; Ephesians 5:3; Matthew 5:28; I Thessalonians 4:3-5; Proverbs 5:15-19; I Corinthians 6:9-20.

82 Luke 1:16, 17; Luke 3.

83 Goyims. *reddit.com*. 1 December 2015. 31 July 2019.

84 Marx, Karl. "marxists.org." 1845. *Theses On Feuerbach*. 17 June 2020.

85 In Greek mythology, King Sisyphus was assigned the eternal task of rolling a heavy stone up a steep hill, only to watch it roll right back down to the bottom again every time he neared the top.

86 Lewis, C.S. *Letters of C.S. Lewis*. Ed. W.H. Lewis and Walter Hooper. HarperOne, 2017. 524.

87 Barton, David and John Cotton. *The New England Primer, Improved for the More Easy Attaining the True Reading of English*. Aledo, TX: WallBuilder Press, 1991, 15th printing 2017.

88 Ibid.

89 Ollman, Bertell. "A Model of Activist Research: How to Study Class Consciousness...and Why We Should." n.d. *nyu.edu*. 7 May 2020. VI.

90 Wallace, Julia and Jimena Vergara. "Black Liberation and the Early Communist Movement." 9 February 2020. *leftvoice.org.* 20 February 2020.

91 Merriam-Webster. *merriam-webster.com.* n.d. 27 June 2020.

92 Lavelle, Kristen M. and Joe Feagin. "Institutional Racism." *encyclopedia.com.* 2 August 2020.

93 Cole, Nicki Lisa. "Definition of Systemic Racism in Sociology." 11 June 2020. *thoughtco.com.* 17 June 2020.

94 Feagin, Joe R. *Systemic Racism: A Theory of Oppression.* New York: Routledge, 2006.

95 Ibid. xii, xiii.

96 Ibid. 24.

97 Ibid. 6.

98 Ibid. 309.

99 Ibid. 310.

100 Feagin, Joe R. *Racist America: Roots, Current Realities, and Future Reparations.* New York and London: Routledge, 2000.

101 Feagin, Joe R. *Systemic Racism: A Theory of Oppression.* New York: Routledge, 2006. 34.

102 Ibid. 46.

103 Ibid. 29, 30.

104 Ibid. 297.

105 Ibid. 318.

106 Ibid. 51, 280.

107 Ibid. 281.

108 Ibid. 25, 26, 307, 308.

109 Ibid. 307.

110 Ibid. 310.

111 Ibid. 311.

112 Ibid. 311.

113 Ibid. 315.

114 Ibid. 321.

115 Ibid. 253.

116 Ibid. 72.

117 Ibid. 29.

118 Ibid. 30.

119 Metaxas, Eric. *Bonhoeffer Pastor, Martyr, Prophet, Spy*. Nashville: Thomas Nelson, 2010. 446.

120 DiLorenzo, Thomas. *The Problem with Socialism*. Washington, DC: Regnery Publishing, 2016. 71.

121 Ibid. 73, 74.

122 Ibid. 114.

123 Ward, Emily. "CDC: 36% of Abortions Abort Black Babies." 28 November 2018. *cnsnews.com*. 17 June 2020.

124 Ibid.

125 I Corinthians 13:6.

126 Romans 3:9-12, 23.

127 Woolston, C. H. *Jesus Loves the Little Children*. 1856-1927.

128 Galatians 6:4, 5; Romans 12:2.

129 Genesis 6:11.

130 Ezekiel 11:19, 36:26; Hebrews 10:22.

131 Ephesians 4:30; 2 Corinthians 1:21, 22.

132 Romans 2:11; Acts 10:34, 35.

133 Carter, Heath W. "Does Socialism Have to Be 'Godless?'" 20 November 2019. *christianitytoday.com*. 24 July 2020.

134 Cook, Vanessa. *Spiritual Socialists: Religion and the American Left*. Philadelphia: University of Pennsylvania Press, 2019.

135 Ibid. 91, 133.

136 Ibid. 220.

137 Ibid. 3683.

138 Ibid. 3699.

139 Ibid. 3731.

140 Ibid. 1627.

141 Ibid. 4511.

142 Carter, Heath W. "Does Socialism Have to Be 'Godless?'" 20 November 2019. *christianitytoday.com.* 24 July 2020.

143 Ibid.

144 Cillizza, Chris. "Bernie Sanders's Liberty University Speech, Annotated." 14 September 2015. *washingtonpost.com.* 15 August 2020.

145 Southern Baptist Convention. "On Critical Race Theory and Intersectionality" 2019. *sbc.net.* 28 July 2020.

146 *By What Standard? God's World...God's Rules.* Founders Ministries. 2019. Digital. (Can be viewed for free at *founders.org/cinedoc/)*

147 Ephesians 6:5-9, I Peter 2:18.

148 Hebrews 12:14.

149 I Timothy 3:1-7, Titus 1:5-9.

150 Hebrews 2:6-9, Luke 12:7, John 3:16.

151 Psalm 139:114; Ephesians 2:10; I Timothy 4:14; I Corinthians 12:7; Romans 12:6-8; I Peter 4:10, 11; Matthew 5:14-16; Matthew 4:19; John 15:8; Galatians 5:16.

152 Brooks, Mick. "An introduction to Marx's Labour Theory of Value." 12 July 2005. *marxist.com.* 24 February 2020.

153 Rose, Tom. *Economics: Principles and Policy.* Mercer: American Enterprise Publications, 1996. 33.

154 Ibid. 52.

155 Caffrey, Maria. "Bread and Roses | The poem, the song, the meaning." 24 September 2018. *busy.org.* 25 February 2020.

156 Cooper, Dana. "Work, Capitalism, and Socialism." 19 September 2013. *marxist.com.* 26 February 2020.

157 North, Gary. "Marx's View of the Division of Labor." 1 January 1969. *fee.org.* 25 February 2020.

158 Ibid.

159 Wesley, John. "The Use of Money." 1703-1791. *whatsaiththescripture.com.* 12 May 2020.

160 Matthew 25:14-30; 2 Thessalonians 3:6, 10, 11; Acts 20:35; Proverbs 10:4, 5; Proverbs 12:11; Proverbs 13:11; Proverbs 14:23; Proverbs 24:30-34; Ecclesiastes 9:10; Ecclesiastes 11:1; Colossians 3:23; Luke 19:13.

161 Exodus 18:13-24, Exodus 20:8, Ecclesiastes 5:18-20, Ecclesiastes 8:15, Ecclesiastes 12:12.

162 Ephesians 5:20, Philippians 2:14, I Thessalonians 5:18.

163 Psalm 18:32, Isaiah 40:31, Isaiah 45:24, I Peter 4:11.

164 Leviticus 19:13, Jeremiah 22:13, James 5:4.

165 Proverbs 6:6-8; Proverbs 13:22; Proverbs 21:5, 20; Proverbs 27:12; Galatians 5:16; Ephesians 4:28; Luke 14:28; Luke 16:11; 2 Timothy 1:7.

166 Proverbs 3:27; Malachi 3:10; Matthew 6:19-21; I Timothy 6:10, 18; Acts 4:34; Luke 6:33; Luke 12:20, 21; Luke 12:33, 34; Philippians 3:7; 2 Corinthians 8:9; 2 Corinthians 9:7.

167 2 Corinthians 9:7.

168 Green Party US. "The Green New Deal." n.d. *gp.org.* 2 April 2020.

169 Carrington, Damian. "Climate Crisis: 11,000 Scientists Warn of 'Untold Suffering'." 5 November 2019. *The Guardian.* 2 March 2020.

170 Timsit, Annabelle. "These Millennials Are Going On 'Birth Strike' Because of Climate Change." 14 April 2019. *qz.com.* 12 March 2020.

171 See our discussion of this in Chapter 9.

172 Proverbs 9:10.

173 Peterson, John. "Climate Struggle is Class Struggle." 31 August 2019. *Socialist Revolution.* 1 March 2020.

174 Idso, C. D. Idso and K. E. "Energy, Carbon Dioxide and Earth's Future." 2020. *CO2science.org.* 12 March 2020.

175 Ibid.

176 Ibid.

177 See *climatechangereconsidered.org.*

178 A full copy of NIPCC's report, titled "Climate Change Reconsidered," as well as summaries of this report, are available to read for free at *heartland.org.*

179 NIPCC. "Climate Change Reconsidered II: Physical Science Summary for Policymakers." 2019. *climatechangereconsidered.org.* 12 March 2020. 4.

180 NIPCC. "Climate Change Reconsidered II: Fossil Fuels Summary for Policymakers." 2019. *climatechangereconsidered.org.* 12 March 2020. 14, 15.

181 *Planet of the Humans.* Dirs. Jeff Gibbs and Michael Moore. 2019. Digital.

182 Hendrickson, Mark. "Climate Change: 'Hoax' Or Crime Of The Century?" 16 September 2012. *forbes.com.* 2 March 2020.

183 *Planet of the Humans.* Dirs. Jeff Gibbs and Michael Moore. 2019. Digital.

184 Ibid.

185 Ibid.

186 Ibid.

187 Ibid.

188 Shafarevich, Igor. *The Socialist Phenomenon.* The United States of America: Gideon House Books, 2019.

189 Jude 1:6.

190 Luke 13:25, 2 Thessalonians 1:9.

191 Luke 16:28, Revelation 20:10.

192 Matthew 8:12, Luke 13:28.

193 Psalm 16:11, John 14:6.

194 Bauer, Walter and Frederick William Danker. *A Greek-English Lexicon of the New Testament and Other Early Christian Literature, Third Edition.* University of Chicago Press, 2001.

195 Merriam-Webster. *merriam-webster.com.* n.d. 3 June 2020.

196 I Samuel 17:49.

197 Keener, Craig. "I will remove your lampstand from its place—Revelation 2:6." January 30 2012. *craigkeener.com.* 9 June 2020.

198 Morson, Gary Saul. "Leo Tolstoy." n.d. *britannica.com.* 3 June 2020.

199 Solzhenitsyn, Aleksandr. *August 1914: A Novel (The Red Wheel I).* New York: Farrar, Straus and Giroux; Reprint Edition, 2014. Loc. 789, 7881-7891.

200 Mahoney, Daniel J. "Solzhenitsyn's Red Wheel." May 2015. *firstthings.com.* 3 June 2020.

201 Metaxas, Eric. *Bonhoeffer Pastor, Martyr, Prophet, Spy.* Nashville: Thomas Nelson, 2010. 195.

202 Ibid. 446.

203 Ibid. 446, 447.

204 Solzhenitsyn, Aleksandr. *August 1914: A Novel (The Red Wheel I).* New York: Farrar, Straus and Giroux; Reprint Edition, 2014. Loc. 8009-8032.

205 Metaxas, Eric. *Bonhoeffer Pastor, Martyr, Prophet, Spy.* Nashville: Thomas Nelson, 2010. 153.

206 Millard, Dr. Catherine. "Preachers and Pulpits of the American Revolution." n.d. *christianheritagemins.org.* 3 June 2020.

207 Solzhenitsyn, Aleksandr. *The Gulag Archipelago Two*. Harper & Row; 1st edition, 1975.

208 Wilde, Robert. "The Russian Revolution of 1917." 16 January 2020. *thoughtco.com*. 4 June 2020.

209 Solzhenitsyn, Aleksandr. *The Gulag Archipelago Two*. Harper & Row; 1st edition, 1975. 597-617.

210 Ibid. 628, 629.

211 Ibid. 615.

212 *Multiplied*. Bear Rinehart and Bo Rinehart. NEEDTOBREATHE. 2014.